LIVERPOOL
BEYOND THE BRINK

LIVERPOOL
BEYOND THE BRINK
THE REMAKING OF A POST-IMPERIAL CITY

Michael Parkinson

LIVERPOOL UNIVERSITY PRESS

First published 2019 by
Liverpool University Press
4 Cambridge Street
Liverpool
L69 7ZU

British Library Cataloguing-in-Publication data
A British Library CIP record is available

978-1-78694-217-3 paperback
978-1-78694-216-6 cased

Typeset by Carnegie Book Production, Lancaster
Printed and bound by Gomer Press, Llandysul, Wales

For Joey – still young but beautiful

Contents

Acknowledgements

I could not have written this book without the support of many colleagues over many years. A lot of its primary evidence comes from conversations – some specifically for this book, some for earlier studies, some more generally – I have had with many people who have played their part in Liverpool life in the last thirty years. I am grateful to all of them. They include: Bill Addy, Joe Anderson, Garry Banks, Dave Backhouse, Denise Barrett-Baxendale, Gideon Ben-Tovim, Marge Ben-Tovim, Sir Howard Bernstein, Sir Michael Bibby, Chris Bliss, Mark Bousfield, Elaine Bowker, Mark Boyle, Tom Bloxham, Julia Bradley, Warren Bradley, Paul Brant, Steve Broomhead, Chris Brown, Michael Brown, Margaret Carney, Andrew Carter, Paul Cherpeau, Andy Churchill, Matthew Cliff, Danny Clare, Greg Clark, Flo Clucas, Ed Cox, Sir Graeme Davies, Phil Davies, Janet Dugdale, Dame Louise Ellman, Mike Emmerich, Sam Evans, Jonathan Falkingham, Chris Farrow, David Fleming, Jim Fox, Mike Gahagan, Catherine Garnell, Jim Gill, Sir Ian Gilmore, Sue Grindrod, Barrie Grunewald, Jon Hague, John Hall, Asif Hamid, Mike Harden, Helen Heap, Sir David Henshaw, Lord Michael Heseltine, Colin Hilton, Rod Holmes, Robert Hough, Charles Hubbard, Sarah Jackson, Tim Johnston, Aidan Kehoe, Richard Kemp, Richard Kenyon, Mark Kitts, Bob Lane, Mark Lawler, Sir Terry Leahy, Sir Richard Leese, Alex Lord, Amanda Lyne, Alastair Machray, Ian Maher, Philip McCann, Claire McColgan, Alison McGovern, Frank McKenna, Sara Wilde McKeown, Peter Moore, Andy Moorhead, Paul Morgan, Rachel Mulhearn, Steve Munby, Edward Murphy, Ian Murphy, Andrea Nixon, Andrew Nolan, Tony Okotie, Crispin Pailing, Mike Palin, David Parr, Charlie Parker, Steve Parry, Roger Phillips, Kirsty Pierce, Geoffrey Piper, Bob Pointing, Rob Polhill, Ian Pollitt, Bob Prattey, Lord John Prescott, Peter Radcliffe, Matt Reed, Tony Reeves, Nick Rice, Eric Robinson, Frank Rogers, Philip Rooney, Dave Roscoe, Steve Rotheram, Mike Shields, Nick Small, Lisa Smith, Eric Sorensen, Paul Spooner, Jenny Stewart, Lord Mike Storey, Greg Stott, Neil Sturmey, David Wade-Smith, David Walker, Tom Walker, Alan Welby, John Whaling, Pete Wilcox, Kate Willard and Ian Wray.

Much of the analytical work that underpins it was undertaken with and by my former colleagues in the European Institute of Urban Affairs. They provided the intellectual guts of this book – as well as great friendship over the years. I owe a huge debt of gratitude to Richard Evans, Richard Meegan, Hilary Russell, Jay Karecha, Mary Hutchins, Gerwyn Jones and Jean Parry. If any credit is due to this work, they share it equally. Two colleagues at Liverpool City Council, Martin

Thompson and Tony Wells, were enormously generous to me with their time and information, as was Nicola Christie at Liverpool LEP. Alex Nurse, my colleague at the University of Liverpool, did the excellent maps. Thanks are also due to Chris and Owain at Belzan for providing refuge during the writing.

I was privileged to be given the time and space to write this book while at the University of Liverpool. For that and for her intellectual and practical support I am particularly indebted to the vice chancellor, Professor Dame Janet Beer. I am also grateful for the encouragement of my colleagues at the Heseltine Institute, in particular Professor Fiona Beveridge, who not only introduced me to Liverpool University Press but also supported the publication financially so it is visually stunning but still affordable. At the Press, I had the best possible editor in Alison Welsby, who has judgement and enthusiasm in equal measure. It is a valuable but rare combination.

Several professional colleagues deserve special mention. I would not have even contemplated writing this book without the encouragement of Ged Fitzgerald. He persuaded me it had to be done – and by me. I am grateful to him for that – at least now that it is finished! John Flamson took on the torch and helped me make it a more expansive work than I had anticipated. I am greatly in his debt. Several colleagues who have been players in the city's story read earlier versions of the manuscript and offered wise advice which made it better than it otherwise would have been. For that I want to thank Alan Chape, Peter Bounds, Max Steinberg, Colin Sinclair, Mark Basnett and Chris Murray. However, despite all this support, any errors of fact or interpretation remain mine alone.

My personal debts are well known and cannot be overstated. Fran has always been and remains the rock on which I stand. And Jessica still amazes me by her achievements and her loyalty to the city where she grew up. I hope they think this result of their support is worthwhile.

All that said, it is still hard to write about Liverpool. The players are animated and opinionated. Many won't agree with what I have written. I can see far too many gaps in the story I have told. Others will see many more. Also, the Liverpool story always changes. By the time this book is published I am certain something else of consequence will have happened. However, you have to put your pen down at some point. I hope I have done justice to at least part of the story of this fascinating city – because I owe Liverpool. It gave me my education, family, friends and career. I am truly grateful for that. And I know I am very lucky indeed to be living through its continuing renaissance.

CHAPTER ONE

What is the Liverpool story and why does it matter?

Beyond the brink – but where is Liverpool going?

Liverpool is an endlessly fascinating, challenging city. It has a grip on people's imaginations in a way few other cities do – nationally or internationally. Everybody – business, government, policy makers, the media, pundits and punters – wants to know what is happening in Liverpool. Is it up, is it down? Is it winning, is it losing? Is it at peace or is it at war? But the irony of Liverpool is that you never quite know where the story is going. Just when you thought a path had been laid out, it changes direction all over again. During the past century the city went from being the second city of the greatest empire the world had ever seen into a post-imperial period of economic decline and political despair. But it emerged phoenix-like as one of the most significant examples of urban renaissance in the UK. Thirty years ago few would have predicted its metamorphosis or even believed it was possible. Its story has many lessons for the external world and even more for Liverpool itself.

Liverpool is different

'The constantly offside city' – Sir Simon Rattle

Liverpool waterfront at dawn
© Robin Weaver/
Alamy Stock Photo

'Liverpool – Threshold to the Ends of the Earth' – Michael O'Mahoney

'Liverpool is the pool of life, it makes to live' – Carl Jung

Liverpool may not be better than, but it is different from, other cities. It is not an English but a Celtic city. As the iconic banner on the Kop at Anfield proclaims, 'We're not English, we're Scousers.' Its cultural blend of poets, philosophers, storytellers, *flâneurs*, comedians and musicians; its wide river and seaport; its history of immigrants and emigrants; its combination of global aspiration and intense local chauvinism – all make it different. It is an aggravating, cosmopolitan, self-regarding, expansive place. Its people are simultaneously big-hearted, open-minded, generous, literate, argumentative and querulous. Liverpool is ever so slightly surreal. That's what makes it interesting – and important. It will always have ups and downs. Economic crashes, buildings and people will come and go. But Liverpool will always be the same. It will always attract the curious and the interesting. They come because they never know where the story is going. That's why it will always be there. That's why, if it didn't exist, we would have to invent it.

This book is an attempt by someone who works in, lives in and cares about Liverpool to make sense of this curious city – and its extraordinary if incomplete renaissance. It tries to capture the essence of the city's recent experience without falling into professional Scouse sentimentality. Despite the attention that the city gets from the national and international media, Liverpool's renaissance story has not been properly told or heard – either inside or outside the city. Partly this is because the city still suffers the consequences of some of its self-imposed problems of the past. But it also suffers from cultural blindness and outsiders' reliance upon outdated clichés and prejudices, often fed and exaggerated by the national media. Some people know a part of what happened and the scale of the changes taking place. But fewer know how and why it happened and who helped or hindered the process. Liverpool's story is how a once great imperial city fallen on hard times is becoming a thoroughly modern city of global aspiration, ambition and achievement. This book tries to show how and why.

How much has Liverpool changed since the 1980s?

I first wrote about Liverpool in the 1980s as the city went into an economic, political and financial tailspin which seemed destined to lead to a fatal, tragic ending. I told the story in *Liverpool on the Brink* in 1985, which showed how the city had got into the mess it had and who was responsible for it. It explained how and why economic failure had led to a financial and political crisis, and how in 1984 Liverpool City Council, led by the hard left Militant Tendency, threatened to bankrupt the city to force a Conservative government to give it more money, and it showed how it had all ended in tears. That book was based on a wealth of conversations with the key players and contained much data about the city's economic and financial position as well as many political anecdotes. It caught the mood of those nationally troubled times and was fashionable for a time. It was also regarded as a fair statement of the city's problems, which also allocated responsibility for them fairly. But essentially *The Brink* was a snapshot of one difficult year in the life of a troubled city. It ended while the crisis was still unravelling. It also ended at a very dark point in the city's history. Like others, I knew it was an unfinished story. But at that point I did not want to continue telling it. Partly I became exhausted by being a player in the continuing disputes in the city about the city. Partly I wanted to look at other cities in other countries rather than the one I lived in. And partly it was too painful to chronicle the city's continuing travails.

So I promised myself that I would not write about Liverpool again until it had stopped being a bad news story and had become a good one. As a result, I resisted for many years overtures to complete the story and to show how the city had emerged from the valley of darkness to reach at least the foothills of the sunny uplands – which it now has. Liverpool is a good news story. I experienced this personally when I realised that the way I was being introduced on public platforms had changed. Before 2008 and Liverpool's European Capital of Culture I was described as coming from Liverpool and, by definition, an expert on urban failure. But this switched almost overnight after 2008, when I was described as coming from Liverpool and, by definition, an expert on urban success. Neither was true. But it made a point to me. I realised that it was the right time for someone to tell the story of how Liverpool had moved beyond the brink. So when the then chief executive of Liverpool City Council, Ged Fitzgerald, said in 2017 that the story had to be finished, and by me, with some misgivings I decided to try. Hence the current book.

From the brink of collapse to the brink of what?

To understand the scale of the transformation that has taken place in the city it is worth quoting the opening lines of *The Brink* where I tried to convey the state of the city in 1985.

Cities are the creatures of economics. They survive as communities if they can cope with the vagaries of economic change. Once economic decline sets in, every aspect of their life is threatened. Liverpool is the perfect illustration of that process, for decline has eaten into the city's economy, society and politics. The story began with the port. It made the city great and in the 19th century gave it more millionaires than any other provincial city. But the port's decline left Liverpool with a legacy that makes economic survival, let alone recovery, problematic at best.[1]

Happily I was wrong. The city has not only survived, it is having a remarkable renaissance. But that's how Liverpool looked to me and many others inside

Liverpool
cityscape
© McCoy Wynne
(mccoywynne.co.uk)

and outside the city in the 1980s. It was in desperate straits – economically, financially, socially and politically. Indeed in 1981, after riots in Toxteth, the Cabinet discussed managing its decline rather than spending any more public money on a failed enterprise. But I think I was right in one other judgement I made at the time in *The Brink*: 'Liverpool now stands at the centre of the economic, social and ideological forces facing British cities. It is a test case of the how the country responds politically to long term urban decline.'[2] I think it still does – but in a much more positive sense!

The city has been through a long and difficult process of change. But arguably it has emerged in better shape economically, socially, physically and politically than for a very long time. During the last decade in particular the Liverpool story has been one of genuine progress from difficult beginnings to increased ambition and achievements. It has generated a more successful civic and political leadership. It has begun to find new economic niches. It has found a new economic self-confidence. A series of major investments, projects and events has improved its self-image and its external image. There have been major infrastructure projects across the city region. World-leading companies have made major investments in it. It has made better use of its indigenous assets with significant growth in some key economic sectors. Liverpool city centre, a key driver of investment and jobs for the whole city region, has been regenerated. The city has a transformed waterfront, a booming port, a massive visitor economy, a hugely improved business district, a far better retail offer, a rapidly developing Knowledge Quarter, continuing investment in and expansion of advanced manufacturing and life sciences. There has been significant investment in new hospitals. The universities are growing and are more engaged in city regional affairs. The benefits of substantial European Commission investment and the

hugely successful European Capital of Culture year in 2008 are still being felt. Liverpool is taking its place as one of the UK's increasingly self-confident city regions, with a big potential contribution to make to the northern and national economy.

Much done but more to do

But there is no point being naïve. There remains much to do. Liverpool's fall took place over several decades and its road back could be a long and winding one. Cities are in fierce competition with each other nationally and internationally to attract talent, private and public investment, infrastructure and prestige projects. Liverpool has not fully exploited some of its economic assets, and some of those assets are relatively weak anyway. Also, the fruits of the city's recent success have been unevenly shared between both people and places. There is an economic and social gap to be closed in the city, and there is still a gap to be closed between Liverpool itself and other cities. In addition, a decade of austerity has challenged some of the progress that Liverpool made during the boom. Nevertheless, the baseline has improved and the trend is upward. Most importantly, the mood among many people, places and economic sectors inside the city is much more positive. The city has a more self-confident, optimistic feel and culture. Increasingly outsiders have begun to recognise that something has changed in Liverpool. It is not where it wants and needs to be yet – in national let alone European or global terms. But the city leaders know this, and self-awareness is at least part of the key to success.

Why does Liverpool's story matter? The role of cities in a global economy

This is not just a local story. The renaissance of Liverpool is part of a wider story about the renaissance of big English cities and must be seen in that context. During the past decade, cities in many countries have emerged from a period of decline to find new economic, political and cultural roles. They are increasingly recognised as the dynamos of national economies, not economic liabilities – 'the wealth of nations'. They are not drags on competitiveness to be bailed out by public funds, but the essential drivers of a modern economy with crucial agglomeration assets in an increasingly globalised world. Some are centres of strategic decision making, exchange and communication. Many have concentrations of intellectual resources in universities and research institutions, which encourage high levels of innovation. Many have achieved substantial physical regeneration, especially of their centres. They have substantial cultural capital, which is an increasingly important source of economic growth and job creation. Many are the benchmark against which UK cities should be measured.

The achievements of the UK's 10 Core Cities[3] in the last fifteen years have confirmed their potential. Even though they do not perform as well as their biggest competitors in Europe, or indeed as well as London, their contribution is already big and with the right investment and policies could be bigger. The economic future of the UK is intimately tied up with the prospects and futures of our leading cities. If they don't work, the economy won't work and we won't work. Their performance is also crucial to the current attempt to rebalance the UK, economically and spatially. Their success will be necessary if we are to compete with countries globally, since cities are becoming the drivers of national success in the twenty-first urban century. My own work on Europe showed that countries that have high-performing cities beyond the capital city also have high-performing or more balanced economies. By contrast, those countries that keep their economic eggs in one basket tend to under-perform and are at potential risk.[4] The UK, because of the institutional, economic and financial dominance of London, is one of the latter. However, the UK has recognised this reality and is, if belatedly and slowly, moving in the other direction. It is moving some responsibilities and powers – if not yet enough resources – out of Whitehall and Westminster directly into the hands of the local players whose economic fate and futures are at stake. It is also starting to operate and govern at a wider scale to reflect the real functional urban economies – the city regional level. These policy changes only underline that a resurgent Liverpool could have an important contribution to make to a more successful UK urban system.

As I wrote this book, I became increasingly clear in my own mind what it is really about. It does discuss Liverpool's economy, but it is not primarily about economics. It talks about politics and politicians, but again they are not its primary focus. It talks about money, but it is not a book about local government finance. It talks about improvements in the physical environment, but it is certainly not about Liverpool's architecture, however impressive that may be, with more Grade 1 listed buildings than any other city outside London. The book is about economic place making. In particular it is about the remaking of a post-imperial city. In the nineteenth century Liverpool was the greatest port in the biggest empire the world had even seen. That imperial reality shaped the place and its people in hugely significant ways. It affected its scale, reach, economic and social structure, politics, culture and attitudes. Liverpool was extroverted; globally connected; economically, culturally and socially diverse; self-confident and adventurous. And it was innovative. It had the first public Medical Officer of Health in Dr Duncan; it had the first public washhouses through the work of Kitty Wilkinson; Jesse Hartley built the first inland dock system to protect its cargoes from the Mersey; it opened the first passenger railway system; it built the first air-conditioned building in its civic masterpiece, St George's Hall; the iconic Liver Building was the first building in the world to be constructed from

Liverpool docks, 1890s
© Chronicle/Alamy Stock Photo

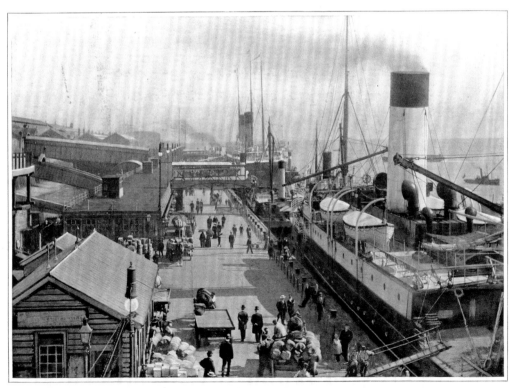

THE LANDING-STAGE. LIVERPOOL (p. 218).

reinforced concrete. But Liverpool was also guilty of making vast fortunes out of the slave trade. And together with its many millionaires there were many more paupers.

When Liverpool began to falter – initially during the great depression of the 1930s but catastrophically after the Second World War as the international terms of trade went against it – many of those characteristics and virtues were challenged and lost. The city became a shadow of its former self economically, politically, socially, culturally and demographically – even though its people and its leaders never really lost the swagger that being an imperial city had brought them. Economically it began to lose its role and self-confidence. Physically the city imploded and disintegrated as it lost almost half its population – 10,000 every year for forty years. Politically it became introverted and resentful. The history of the past three decades can be seen as an attempt to come to terms with those hard realities and to remake a former imperial city into a sustainable post-imperial city, capitalising upon its extraordinary heritage but actively shaping its future. Slowly but surely, like a great jigsaw puzzle, the city is being put together again into a coherent place – economically, physically, politically, socially and culturally. It is not yet done, but the force is with it.

'The story of regeneration in Liverpool is the story of the rise and fall and rise again of the city centre' – Edward Murphy, former chief executive, Liverpool Council for Voluntary Services

This book looks at how economic decline caused the physical, social and political fragmentation of that huge imperial city during the 1970s – and at the efforts since then to revive and reconnect the parts of a disintegrating city. Many of the policies I describe in this book have been attempts to rebuild areas physically, but as part of an effort to make them economically viable again. The geographical focus has shifted over time. Initially the focus was on the waterfront, then the city centre fringe, then part of south Liverpool and more recently the city centre core. Real progress has been made. The city has become a more coherent – if not yet completed – place. Its challenge is to deepen the existing improvements and to extend them to those parts and people who have not yet shared enough in the city's renaissance.

To help the reader see what was happening where during this period, Map 1 shows the most important regeneration initiatives that were introduced across the whole of the city from the 1980s to 2018 and that are discussed in this book. Map 2 focuses on the city centre, where as can be seen very clearly, the bulk of the policy initiatives were located during this period. As we shall see, the initiatives were big, important and effective – but heavily concentrated in the city centre.

It is worth saying at this stage that there are three big areas of the city that need to be addressed in future, but for rather different reasons. One is primarily because of its huge need, the other two because of their huge opportunity.

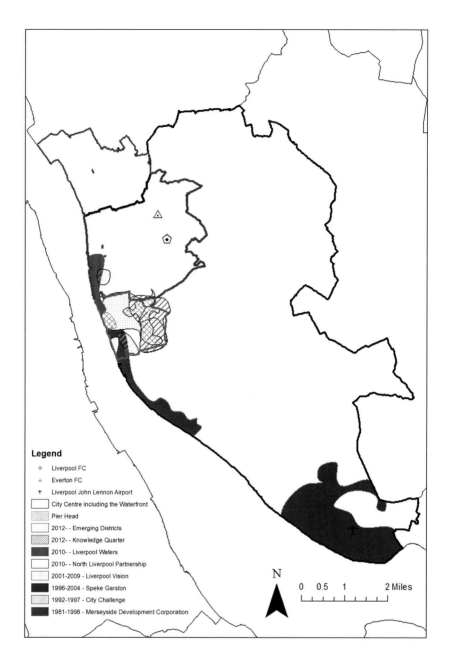

Map 1. Major
regeneration
projects,
Liverpool city
(Crown Copyright,
2018)

Legend

⊕ Liverpool FC
△ Everton FC
✝ Liverpool John Lennon Airport
▢ City Centre including the Waterfront
▨ Pier Head
▢ 2012- - Emerging Districts
▨ 2012- - Knowledge Quarter
■ 2010- - Liverpool Waters
▢ 2010- - North Liverpool Partnership
▢ 2001-2009 - Liverpool Vision
■ 1996-2004 - Speke Garston
▨ 1992-1997 - City Challenge
■ 1981-1998 - Merseyside Development Corporation

N

0   0.5   1   2 Miles

The first is north Liverpool, which was devastated by the decline of the port and docks, has not had the consistent attention given to other areas, and lags behind the rest of the city economically, socially and physically. The planned development of the near north docks and Liverpool Waters and their connection to the area's two anchor football clubs will be crucial to its future prospects. The second area is Knowledge Quarter Liverpool, which is on the edge of the city centre and contains its universities, hospitals and major cultural institutions. This is developing rapidly and could become a key driver of the whole city

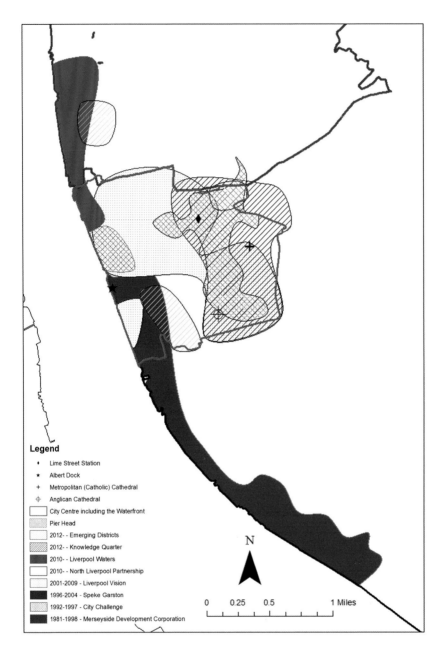

Map 2. Major
regeneration
projects,
Liverpool city
centre
(Crown Copyright,
2018)

Legend

- ◆ Lime Street Station
- ★ Albert Dock
- + Metropolitan (Catholic) Cathedral
- ⊕ Anglican Cathedral
- City Centre including the Waterfront
- Pier Head
- 2012- - Emerging Districts
- 2012- - Knowledge Quarter
- 2010- - Liverpool Waters
- 2010- - North Liverpool Partnership
- 2001-2009 - Liverpool Vision
- 1996-2004 - Speke Garston
- 1992-1997 - City Challenge
- 1981-1998 - Merseyside Development Corporation

N

0   0.25   0.5   1 Miles

regional economy during the next decade. The third area is the city centre, including the waterfront. It is crucial that development here is well planned and of the right quality so that Liverpool retains its character and authenticity and does not, by having too much or the wrong kind of development, pay the price of success in the future as it has paid the price of failure in the past. All these areas will need to succeed if Liverpool is to become a successful, sustainable city, punching its weight in the northern, national and international economy. The risks and opportunities are finely balanced as we shall see later in this book.

This book – like its predecessor which it is intended to update – is meant to be serious and well evidenced but accessible to a wide audience rather than just the academic community. As its original proponent described it, it is a commentary upon the life and times of a city during the past thirty years by someone who has lived through and tried to make sense of them. It is inevitably partial, particular and flawed. But it is the best I can do. It is not easy to write contemporary economic and political history. The narrative is contested. Often neither it nor the events have yet been written down. They are both constantly shifting. It is definitely easier to write about decline and fall in the past than about continuing renaissance in the present. As another former chief executive of the city, Peter Bounds, said to me: 'Your problem, Michael, is that *Liverpool on the Brink* was about one difficult year in the life of the city. This is about thirty years of continuing progress. How are you going to tell it?'

My answer is that I shall focus on what to me at least seem to be the main issues. And I will concentrate on what I know rather than what I don't know. Liverpool is a big place with many big stories, and in this book I cannot attempt to tell all of them, no matter how important they are. For example, I do not go into great detail about many of the challenges and complexities that Liverpool faces in its schools, health, housing, welfare, transport or policing systems – or more controversially, the scale and impact of the city's drug economy or the challenges it faces in its racial and community relations. Others are far better qualified than me to fill the many such gaps in events or understanding that I will inevitably leave. And I certainly do not have all the answers to the questions that this book raises. I regard that as the collective responsibility of the city's leadership and its people, rather than of an observer of the city's condition. I also have to resolve the classic dilemma when writing about Liverpool – are you Pollyanna or Eeyore? Do you talk the place up or talk it down? Will the locals even agree about whether you are being too optimistic or too pessimistic? My experience is that they will not. So my solution is to try to be as honest as possible and tell the story impartially but constructively.

The book draws on three kinds of evidence. The first is what other people have written about the city over the years. There is a burgeoning literature about Liverpool's past and present performance. For example, Tristram Hunt's *Ten Cities that Made an Empire* underlines the significance of Liverpool's imperial past and present, as does Tony Lane's *Liverpool: Gateway to Empire*.[5] They both influenced my choice of title for this book. Ronaldo Munck's collection *Reinventing the City: Liverpool in Comparative Perspective* delves into its economic and social decline and renaissance until the beginning of the twenty-first century, with especially important contributions from Richard Meegan and Stuart Wilks Heeg.[6] John Belchem's collection *Liverpool 800: Culture, Character and History* reflects on the changing character and culture of the city over its 800 years, with an especially thorough review of the post-1945 period by Jon Murden.[7] Chris Crouch's *City of Change and Challenge* is a very detailed history of the regeneration of the city seen through the prism of the changing UK planning system.[8] Matthew Cocks's PhD thesis 'Institutional Thickness and Liverpool' provides a valuable discussion of the many regeneration initiatives that Liverpool has experienced since the 1970s, and of the people and organisations that contributed most to its continuing renaissance.[9] Olivier Sykes et al.'s 'A City Profile of Liverpool' is a very helpful overview of the main periods since the turn of the century, as is Olivier Sykes and David Shaw's 'Liverpool Story' in *Transforming Distressed Global Communities*.[10] Diane Frost and Peter North's *Militant Liverpool* and Michael Crick's *The March of Militant* dug deeply into the city's political travails during the 1980s.[11] They are all important sources of evidence, analysis and argument for this book which I wish to fully acknowledge. Other more detailed research is identified in later chapters.

My second evidence source is the work I have done with my former colleagues in the European Institute for Urban Affairs on the Liverpool story, as well as that of other UK and European cities. *The Brink* first told the story of the city's decline, as did my essays on aspects of Liverpool's leadership, regeneration, money and culture in *Regenerating the Cities: The UK Crisis and the American Experience, Leadership and Urban Regeneration: Cities in North America and Europe, Cultural Policy and Urban Regeneration: The West European Experience* and *European Cities Towards 2000*.[12] I first started to tell the story of the unfolding renaissance of Liverpool during the boom years of the 2000s in *Make No Little Plans* in 2008.[13] I continued with work on the city's economy and politics during the recent period of austerity, including *The State of Liverpool City Region Report, Liverpool's Elected Mayor 2012–16* and *Albert Dock: What Part in Liverpool's Continuing Renaissance?*[14] Other more general work I did with colleagues on cities and urban policy in the UK and Europe helped me to place Liverpool's renaissance in a wider context. That work includes *City Matters – Competitiveness, Cohesion and Urban Governance, Competitive European Cities: Where Do the Core Cities Stand?, The State of English Cities Report, Second Tier Cities* and *UK City Regions in Growth and Recession*.[15]

My third source of evidence is a series of extended conversations I have had with individuals who played key roles in the city during the past thirty years. I have interviewed over 100 of them in recent years for my work on the city's renaissance, many although not all specifically for this book. They provide an important insight into the shifting moods of the city, its people and its leaders during the past thirty years. I draw extensively on their views throughout the book to show their state of mind – then and now. And I quote directly from many of these interviews throughout this book.

I agonised about the best way of telling the story – in particular whether I should tell it thematically or chronologically. In the end I adopted a broad chronological approach which I thought was needed to give the reader enough detail to be able to understand the changes the city has been through. I have periodised the past forty years in a way that gives some sense of the main epochs. I call the 1970s and early 1980s 'the age of coalition and paralysis', when no political party controlled and ran the city council, and so it failed to address its looming economic crisis. As a result the city drifted towards a political crisis. 'The age of confrontation and chaos' is the period from 1983 to 1987 when Militant Labour ran the city and tried to exploit Liverpool's economic and financial travails using the threat of municipal bankruptcy to bring down a national government. It failed badly, and the city paid a very heavy price. 'The age of normalisation' covers 1988–98, as a reformed if still divided Labour Party tried to pick up the pieces left by its Militant predecessor and to make the city function normally once again. 'The rise of the aspiring premier European city' was the period from 1998 to 2010 when the Liberal Democrat Party built on the foundations of Labour's normalisation but pursued a much more ambitious strategy to make Liverpool a major player on the national and wider European stage. It put Liverpool back in the news for the right reasons. 'Continuing ambition in an age of austerity, 2010–19' describes the ruling Labour Party's and elected mayor's attempt to keep Liverpool on its path to recovery despite the impact of the global recession, nationally imposed austerity and growing financial problems. These eras were not self-contained. Inevitably each influenced for better or worse those that were to follow. And this periodisation does oversimplify a little who did what and what happened when. But I think it helps us to see the tectonic plates shift as Liverpool fell and rose again.

How have I organised the book?

I have divided the book into six substantive chapters. In them I try to answer a common set of questions, lengthier versions of the only questions that really matter in life – how did we get here and where are we going next? They include: How far has Liverpool come and where does it now stand in comparison with thirty years ago, and also in comparison with other big cities in the UK? What were the most important forces driving change? Who helped most and least – local politicians, business, community leaders, national politicians, government, Europe? Who gained most and least – which people and which places? Finally I ask, what's next for Liverpool?

Chapter 2, 'Liverpool goes on – but pulls back from – the brink, 1973–88', describes how the economic decline of a great former imperial city combined with fiscal stress and the threat of bankruptcy almost led it into political chaos, with national government taking direct control of the city. But it also tells how in the end that fate was narrowly averted. During the 1960s and early 1970s Liverpool still had a powerful maritime and manufacturing base, ambitious plans to modernise the city centre and genuine prospects of economic resurgence. However, that changed during the 'lost decade' of 1973–83 as the city went through a period of coalition politics and confusion and lacked the strategic leadership needed to face up to the consequences of the 1973 oil shocks and global recession. That period sowed the seeds of what was to come in the age of confrontation and chaos from 1983 to 1987. Then a Militant Labour controlled city council attempted to blackmail with the threat of municipal bankruptcy the free market government of Margaret Thatcher as it began to remove the public-sector leg of the Liverpool economy just as its private-sector leg was buckling. It all ended in tears as Militant were thrown out of the council and the Labour Party. The city pulled back from the brink of fiscal and political collapse and began to develop a different economic and political strategy that would play to some of its strengths and capitalise upon some of its assets, especially the economy of the city centre.

Chapter 3 I call 'Liverpool begins to become normal, 1988–98', as the city's political and business classes, led by a moderate but still divided Labour Party, desperately attempted to bring the city further back from the brink and to reposition it as normal city that could manage its services efficiently, work with the government and the private sector, get its economy going again and put Liverpool on the back rather than the front pages of the national press. Although

Protest in support of Liverpool Labour Council, 1986
© Dave Sinclair

the city did not meet all those challenges and the leadership ran out of steam politically, it made some important progress. Through a series of successful initiatives funded by Europe and national government it put in place some important building blocks for progress across the city – on the waterfront, the edge of the city centre and in the south of the city. And it improved relationships between the city council, the private sector and national government. It began the remaking of the post-imperial city. And in doing so it laid the foundations for the better things that were to follow.

Chapter 4 is 'The rise of the aspiring premier European city, 1998–2010'. In this now golden age for the city, a Liberal Democrat administration successfully combined the New Labour government's commitment to cities and public expenditure, revived private-sector interest in city-centre investment, and large amounts of European money to make dramatic physical, economic and cultural changes that dragged Liverpool into the mainstream of national and European cities. It was a hugely successful period for Liverpool economically, politically, culturally, physically and psychologically – spearheaded by a city-centre regeneration organisation vehicle, Liverpool Vision, and symbolised by its extraordinarily successful European Capital of Culture year in 2008.

Chapter 5 is 'Continuing ambition in an age of austerity, 2010–19'. Liverpool had a very good boom, closing the gap with some other UK and European cities, until austerity hit after 2008. Although austerity did not completely arrest an era of continuing civic ambition, it did constrain it. During this period the political leadership of the city tried to ride two horses and cope with large cuts in government funding to the city while continuing the policies of economic modernisation, working in partnership with government and the private sector rather than retreating to the confrontational tactics of the 1980s. For a city that had become associated with turbulent and truculent politics and that faced greater financial challenges than it had in the 1980s, its leadership demonstrated an impressive degree of pragmatism. Also the wider non-political and private leadership of the city increasingly stepped up to the plate. National policies that encouraged city regional economic and political leadership also began to make a difference. In 2019, despite the challenges it faced, the city was arguably more productive, better governed, more self-confident and outward-looking than it had been for many years.

Chapter 6, 'The state of Liverpool's economy today', moves beyond politics, policy and personalities to the fundamentals of the city and city region economy. It assesses how far Liverpool's economy has come in the past thirty years. Given where it was in the 1980s, the city has had an extraordinary if incomplete renaissance. It is a fundamentally different economy with many strengths, major and minor. But despite its many achievements, Liverpool still faces very large challenges if it is to sustain its recent successes. The city is well off its knees, as the Scousers would say, but not yet out of the woods. The chapter discusses the drivers of a city's success – innovation, skills, diversity, connectivity, place quality

Sea Odyssey:
Giant
Spectacular,
2012
Image reproduced
by permission of
Culture Liverpool,
Liverpool City
Council

and strategic capacity – and assesses in some detail Liverpool's economic and social performance in terms of those drivers.

Chapter 7, 'Liverpool beyond the brink: what are the lessons and what is to be done?', pulls the threads of the narrative together. It does three things. First, it identifies the secrets of and messages from Liverpool's renaissance in the past thirty years. Secondly, it reflects upon the contribution of key individuals involved in remaking a post-imperial city. Finally, it identifies a series of challenges that the city will face in the future. They are economic, social, cultural and political. They are not only the result of the price of failure, the city's traditional problem, but ironically of the potential price of success. For example, European programmes and money are not available now at the scale they were when Liverpool began its renaissance. National government urban policies, which played such an important part in encouraging the city's renaissance, have been reduced. The fiscal challenges for the city council in particular are greater than those faced by Militant in the 1980s. The challenges of a socially and economically uneven and divided city remain. The rise of Momentum in the Labour Party may yet affect the future leadership and pattern of politics across the whole one-party-controlled city region. The scale, nature and quality of the development that is now taking place in the city could affect its traditional authenticity. And the spectre of Brexit looms over it as over every other big city in the UK. The chapter spells out what Liverpool leaders should do to capitalise upon the city's recent success and exploit the many opportunities it faces. It asks who needs to do what better or differently in future. And it asks what kind of city and for whom Liverpool should aim to be anyway. It identifies the three key areas of the city that its leaders have to deliver upon next – Knowledge Quarter Liverpool, north Liverpool and the city centre and waterfront. It also identifies the three big themes its leaders will need to work harder on if Liverpool is to be a successful post-imperial city – productivity, place and people. Liverpool needs better jobs for more people, development that is authentic and high quality and a fairer distribution of the fruits of its growing success.

Who is the book for?

There are messages for different audiences in this book – at home and abroad.

So what for national government?
There are important lessons for government. These partly concern the role of big cities such as Liverpool and their contribution to the national economy and raise the question whether national government has sufficiently recognised the scale of the potential contribution of such cities outside London. Different governments adopted different policies at different times and I ask whether their priorities, resources and organisation helped or hindered Liverpool's continuing renaissance – then and now. In fact many of the projects that kick-started Liverpool's recovery were created and financed by national government as well as by the European Commission. So public intervention has been crucial. There are also many detailed lessons about how and why public interventions and initiatives worked well at difficult times in Liverpool that government would do well to remember in future, as it equivocates in its attitudes to our cities outside London.

So what for an international audience?
There is also a wider international audience for this book, with messages for cities in countries with different systems but with similar pasts and prospects. One of the key features of Liverpool is that it is well known and probably better loved outside the UK than it is inside. Partly this is because of its imperial past, its maritime history and its outward-facing culture. In part it is because of its waterfront, music and football. And in part it is because of the different character of its people. There is a greater appetite abroad to understand what has been happening in Liverpool and a willingness to see more of its virtues and fewer of its vices than there is in the domestic, London-centric political and financial bubble. It is an exaggeration but not wholly untrue to argue that, even today,

it is easier to tempt investors to travel from Asia or America than to get them on the two-hour train journey from London Euston. In these Brexit days there are also important lessons about Europe that contributed greatly to the city's renaissance. Europe's money but also the challenge it put to the city's leaders – what will Liverpool be for in future? – was hugely significant in helping the city to help itself at a time when national government was much less willing to take a risk and invest in the city. The particular features of its success may be *sui generis*, but Liverpool's recovery does provide messages for post-industrial cities trying to develop new roles and relationships in an increasingly competitive and unstable global world.

So what for the Scousers?

Some of the biggest messages are for the people and businesses of Liverpool and its city region. The most obvious one is that the city has turned the corner. It is not going back to the bad old days, even if it has more challenges ahead. It is also clear that the virtues and qualities it has shown recently of confidence, ambition, leadership, partnership, trust and delivery will serve it better than the pessimism and introversion of the culture of failure that developed during the dark and difficult days of the 1980s. There is a huge amount to build on. But the greatest risk to cities is complacency. There is certainly no room for complacency in Liverpool. But the key message for the Scousers is that we have shown to ourselves and others our better face in the last ten years. We have realised that the city is a gift that has to be nourished and cherished. And we have begun to do so. As a great leader once said, the only thing to fear is fear itself. Liverpool has no need to fear for the future – as I hope the rest of this book will show.

Notes

1   Michael Parkinson, *Liverpool on the Brink: One City's Struggle Against Government Cuts* (Policy Journals, 1985), p. 10.

2   Parkinson, *Liverpool on the Brink*, p. 9.

3   The UK Core Cities are Birmingham, Bristol, Cardiff, Glasgow, Leeds, Liverpool, Manchester, Newcastle, Nottingham and Sheffield.

4   Michael Parkinson, Richard Meegan, Jay Karecha and Richard Evans, *Second Tier Cities: In an Age of Austerity Why Invest Outside the Capitals?* (ESPON, 2012); Michael Parkinson and Richard Meegan, 'Economic Place Making: Policy Messages for European Cities', *Policy Studies*, 34.3 (2013); Michael Parkinson, *No Cities, No Civilisation: No Successful Cities, No Successful Nations* (Core Cities, 2013).

5   Tristram Hunt, *Ten Cities that Made an Empire* (Allen Lane, 2014); Tony Lane, *Liverpool: Gateway of Empire* (Lawrence and Wishart, 1987).

6   Ronaldo Munck (ed.), *Reinventing the City: Liverpool in Comparative Perspective* (Liverpool University Press, 2003).

7   Jon Murden, '"City of Change and Challenge": Liverpool since 1945', in John Belchem (ed.), *Liverpool 800: Culture, Character and History* (Liverpool University Press, 2006).

8   Chris Crouch, *City of Change and Challenge: Urban Planning and Regeneration in Liverpool* (Ashgate, 2003).

9   Matthew Cocks, 'Institutional Thickness and Liverpool', PhD thesis, University of Liverpool, 2010.

10 Olivier Sykes et al., 'A City Profile of Liverpool', *Cities*, 35 (2013), https://doi.org/10.1016/j.cities.2013.03.013 (accessed 26 December 2018); David Shaw and Olivier Sykes, 'Liverpool Story: Growth, Distress, Reinvention, and Place-Based Strategy in a Northern City', in Fritz Wagner,

Riad Mahayni and Andreas G. Piller (eds), *Transforming Distressed Global Communities: Making Inclusive, Safe, Resilient, and Sustainable Cities* (Routledge, 2016).

11 Diane Frost and Peter North, *Militant Liverpool: A City on the Edge* (Liverpool University Press, 2013); Michael Crick, *The March of Militant* (Faber and Faber, 1984).

12 Michael Parkinson, Bernard Foley and Dennis Judd (eds), *Regenerating the Cities: The UK Crisis and the American Experience* (Manchester University Press, 1988); Michael Parkinson and Dennis Judd (eds), *Leadership and Urban Regeneration: Cities in North America and Western Europe* (Sage, 1990); Franco Bianchini and Michael Parkinson (eds), *Cultural Policy and Urban Regeneration: The West European Experience* (Manchester University Press, 1993); Michael Parkinson, with Alan Harding et al. (eds), *European Cities Towards 2000: Profiles, Policies and Prospects* (Manchester University Press, 1994).

13 Michael Parkinson, *Make No Little Plans: The Regeneration of Liverpool City Centre* (Liverpool Vision, 2008).

14 Michael Parkinson and Alex Lord, *Albert Dock: What Part in Liverpool's Continuing Renaissance?* (Heseltine Institute, University of Liverpool, 2016).

15 Martin Boddy and Michael Parkinson, *City Matters – Competitiveness, Cohesion and Urban Governance* (Policy Press, 2004); Michael Parkinson, Mary Hutchinson, James Simmie, Greg Clark and Hans Verdonk, *Competitive European Cities: Where Do the Core Cities Stand?* (ODPM, 2004); Michael Parkinson et al., *The State of English Cities Report* (ODPM, HMSO, 2006); Michael Parkinson, Richard Meegan and Jay Karecha, *UK City Regions in Growth and Recession* (ESRC, 2014).

LIVERPOOL CITY COUNCIL
ELECTIONS MAY 6TH
MARXISTS
OUT
LIBERALS
IN
LONG
LANE L15

Liverpool goes on – but pulls back from – the brink, 1973–88

A changing economy and a changing polity

This chapter looks at the way in which, during the 1970s and 1980s, Liverpool came to the brink of economic and political collapse but managed to pull back from it. In this period the rapid decline of the city's traditional port and manufacturing industries, the election of a Conservative government determined to cut public expenditure, and the peculiarities of the city's social structure and politics combined to throw Liverpool into confrontation and near chaos. The chapter outlines how economic decline and its impact upon social problems led a Militant Tendency controlled Labour council to self-destruct in a very public confrontation with national government. It also shows how that experience alarmed and frightened many inside the city and led to a gradual change in its politics, culture and policies. The period started with confusion and confrontation and ended in a degree of public and political consensus that a new approach to the future of the city was needed. But the consensus was fragile and the city still faced many economic, institutional and political challenges.

There were three major phases of political life in the city in this period, which produced three different local economic strategies. The period 1973–83 witnessed a dramatic escalation of the city's economic problems, combined with a period of political paralysis because none of the city's three political parties could achieve the necessary support to get a majority on the council and develop a coherent response to economic decline. The period 1983–87 was marked by the rise of a powerful Labour majority on the city council which regarded a major public spending programme on the physical infrastructure of its working-class heartland as the only way to regenerate

Economic crisis in England in the 1980s; election billboard in Liverpool on 24 February 1983
Photo by Jacob SUTTON/ Gamma-Rapho via Getty Images

Liverpool's economy. Labour's strategy during this period alienated the Conservative government and the local private sector and ended in political and legal defeat for Labour. After 1987, as the failure of Labour's strategy became apparent to all political actors in the city, an alternative development strategy began to emerge. During this crucial period, changes of political leadership and strategies in the public and private sectors meant that the city's politics began to change from municipal socialism to urban entrepreneurialism. A Labour regime emerged that was eager to form alliances with the local private sector and pursue an economic development strategy more in tune with the priorities of national government.[1]

The fall of an imperial maritime economy

'Liverpool was just magical. I remember going down to the docks with my dad in the early 60s. It was a hive of activity. It was a frenzy of cargo, ships, tugs, cranes, the overhead railway – the whole world was in action at the docks in Liverpool.' – Robert Hough, former chair Liverpool City Region LEP

Liverpool had a dramatic rise to economic power, and an equally dramatic if faster fall from power. It went from being the second city of the largest empire the world had ever known during the late nineteenth century into one of the poorest city regions in Europe by the late twentieth century. As Richard Meegan has argued, Liverpool was at the peak of its economic power at the turn of the twentieth century, a power symbolised in the bricks and mortar of its 'Three Graces', the three world-famous waterfront buildings at the Pier Head, which were started in 1906 and finished in 1917. But as he also pointed out, while these buildings were being erected the world was changing, the international division of labour was changing, and with it Liverpool's role. The Liverpool story began with the port, but the port's decline created huge problems in the post-war period. The port dominated Liverpool's economy, and throughout the nineteenth century the city flourished on it. But the city's over-dependence on the port made it vulnerable to change. Its fall began with the depression of the 1930s. But changes in the international and national economy after the war dramatically speeded up that process, sending the port into a long-term decline with profound effects upon its economy and causing long-term structural unemployment.[2]

The port also shaped the structure of the local economy, creating substantial dependence on semi-skilled jobs and blue-collar service-sector jobs in the city. The relative absence of a manufacturing base and a white-collar service sector meant that the city was poorly positioned to expand into those sectors to compensate for the decline of port-related work. During the depression of the 1930s, unemployment in Liverpool rose to 28% and was always one and a half times greater than the national average. In the late 1940s it rose to over two and a half times the national average. Government policies in the 1950s did bring some new manufacturing jobs to the city, but other factory closures and the loss of jobs in the port cancelled them out. The 1960s promised better things for the city as government policy to redistribute industry with an investment programme of £65 million brought 25,000 jobs. For the first time in its history, in the early 1960s manufacturing became a growth sector in Merseyside. By the end of the decade there was view that the place was on the road to recovery. But the flirtation with manufacturing did not continue, and the gains of the 1960s were not sustained because of the economic shocks caused by the coming global recession.

The long-term decline of the economy was dramatically escalated after 1973 by two economic forces – the recession that resulted from the oil crisis, and Britain's entry into the European Common Market. The latter weakened the Atlantic-facing west coast port. The former sent shock waves through many of the city's large, externally controlled firms. During the next decade a process of disinvestment, contraction and closures sent the city's economy into a tailspin. During this period 60,000 jobs were lost and unemployment rose to 27%, twice the national average. Employment in the city region had peaked in the mid-1960s, but there was relentless decline thereafter, most dramatically in the late 1970s and early 1980s. Between 1966 and 1978 the city lost 20% of its jobs, a much bigger proportion than the national, regional and city-regional losses. Three hundred and fifty plants closed or transferred production elsewhere, with the loss of 40,000 jobs. At the same time the port continued its decline. Its share of total imports and exports was almost halved from 15% to 8% and its workforce reduced to 3,000 from the 25,000 it had been in 1945. It got much worse after 1978. Between 1978 and 1991, 37% of jobs disappeared – almost 9,000 jobs a year. The local economy was devastated. Unemployment soared and outmigration accelerated.

A crucial problem for the city was that it was a branch plant economy. Its economy was dominated by large employers, often externally controlled. Less than 1% of firms provided 40% of the city's jobs. In 1985 only 1 in 20 of the largest manufacturing plants was locally controlled. Such firms had little loyalty to the place and were vulnerable to rationalisation and restructuring during recession. And such losses tended to wipe out any gains in the small-firm sector of the economy. At that time seven big firms controlled over half the manufacturing jobs, and between 1981 and 1985 they shed 30% of their jobs. The decline of manufacturing was not compensated for by increases in the service sector, which grew, but below the national rate and mainly in public-sector jobs. Between 1971 and 1985 total employment in the city fell by 33%. Unemployment reflected the change. During the 1970s unemployment rose from 5% to 20%. By 1985 it was 27% – double the national average. Liverpool appeared to have lost control of its economic destiny.[3]

'In the 80s if you were working in business outside of Liverpool you simply couldn't bring a proposal to your board to invest in Liverpool. You would get laughed out of the room.' – Sir Terry Leahy, former CEO Tesco, and former board member, Liverpool Vision

Urban riots, Toxteth 1981

As it entered the 1980s the city was in danger of becoming socially and economically polarised, with unpredictable consequences. In 1981 the city's planning officer reported that 'the extreme variations within the city in terms of unemployment, job prospects and income levels – could have a detrimental and lasting effect on its social and economic fabric'.[4] That report proved prophetic. In July 1981 a furious bout of rioting, looting and arson broke out in the inner-city area of Toxteth, the home of some of the poorest black and white people in the city. Police were drafted in from across the country and tear gas was used for the first time on the British mainland to control some of the worst pitched battles. The riots had been started initially by police attempting to arrest a local black youth, but this set alight simmering resentments between the local black population and the police. The insurrection spread to whites as the dispossessed of the inner city rose in a poor people's revolt against authority. At the end of two weeks of sporadic violence, a young man was dead, hundreds of police and

Toxteth riots,
12 July 1981
© Keystone Pictures
USA/Alamy Stock
Photo

unknown numbers of civilians had been injured and millions of pounds' worth of damage had been unleashed upon the neighbourhood's public buildings, homes and shops. And a government had been frightened.

As Michael Heseltine's 'It took a riot' memo to the Cabinet underlined, the government only began to take seriously the problems of the poorest city in Britain when they threatened public order.[5] After the tear gas had dispersed and a bevy of ministers and private-sector leaders had toured the battle zone, it came up with a new initiative – a Minister for Merseyside, Michael Heseltine, and a new administrative unit, the Merseyside Task Force, consisting of civil servants from three government departments and private secondees.[6] In fact, the Task Force attracted some talented people who were committed to the city. Together they began some of the early regeneration projects in Liverpool, including Wavertree Technology Park, the International Garden Festival and the Stockbridge Village initiative. At different times the directors of the Merseyside Task Force played important roles, encouraging Liverpool to change but still promoting its case in London to their political and administrative masters. Three in particular stood out – Eric Sorensen, David Bradley and Bob Dobbie. They all 'got' Liverpool and were in various ways friends at court for the city. But the scale of the Task Force's activities did not match the scale of the need. And it could not prevent the political crisis that was to come. Heseltine subsequently wrote of those times in the early 1980s:

Alone every night, when the meetings were over and the pressure was off, I would stand every evening with a glass of wine looking out at the magnificent view over the river and ask myself what had gone wrong with this great English city. The Mersey, its lifeblood, flowed as majestically as ever down from the hills. Its monumental Georgian and Victorian buildings, created with such pride and at such cost by the city fathers of a century before and earlier, still dominated the skyline. The Liver Building itself, the epicentre of a trading system that reached the four corners of the earth, stood defiant and from my perspective very alone. The port had serviced an empire and sourced a world trade. But in truth everything had gone wrong.[7]

Economic decline poisons politics and creates instability

Economic decline dramatically affected the city's politics and civic life during the 1970s and 1980s. A series of economic, institutional and political pressures pushed Liverpool towards the brink of financial and political chaos. These included the collapse of its externally controlled economy as companies disinvested and restructured during an internal recession; the election of a Conservative government with an ideological distaste for the public sector and a commitment to the private sector; the introduction of a controversial government grant system designed to impose fiscal austerity; intense ideological disputes and chaotic political responses to the city's economic decline; and finally the radicalisation of the Liverpool Labour Party and key municipal unions. The decline of the private sector during the 1970s was partly compensated for by the fact that employment in the public-sector city was growing. Expansion in central and local government, the health services, the university, the police and the nationalised industries masked the contraction of the private sector. However, when national government policy changed in the late 1970s, first under the impact of Labour's austerity programme and later because of the Conservative government's commitment to reduce the public sector, the vulnerability of the city's economy was fully revealed. This had a major impact upon the city's politics, in particular exaggerating conflict between its political parties about how Liverpool should respond to the combined effect of national policies and economic decline. The cuts in public-sector expenditure especially encouraged the Liverpool Labour Party to the left and towards a direct confrontation with the national government. In turn this reinforced the divide between the local private sector and local politicians.

If 1973 had been a major turning point in Liverpool's economy, it was also of great political significance. The restructuring of its electoral boundaries that year helped to produce a major political upheaval, as a minority Liberal Party, which had previously held no more than a few seats on the city council, emerged to take control from the Labour and Conservative parties, which had traditionally dominated the city. But the Liberals never achieved an overall majority on the council and there was a period of weak and divided coalition government between Liberals and Conservatives until the beginning of the 1980s. There were constant hung councils, minority and coalition administrations and political confusion. The Liberals' focus upon the private sector, combined with its efforts to reduce the scale of public-sector housing and reduce local taxes, created intense hostility from the Labour Party. For much of the time partisan conflict over the minutiae of party politics and bitter competition between the parties to secure their volatile electoral support distracted attention from the larger issues of economic decline. This meant that the city lacked the capacity to confront the fiscal, administrative and social consequences of its rapid economic decline. It failed to take a series of difficult decisions to rationalise the management and financing of the city. Politicians were unable or unwilling to confront the power of the blue-collar trade unions, which represented many council employees, and did not begin the rationalisation of the city's basic services. The council was unable to modernise its machinery, which became outdated and inefficient. Liverpool drifted through a crucial decade of economic decline with little clear response to it.

The Liberal administration of the 1970s had two major policy ambitions. The first was to dismantle the large municipal housing stock that had been built up by the Labour and Conservative councils in the 1950s and 1960s.[8] The second was to reduce the level of rates to encourage the private sector to remain in the

city. It was essentially a supply-led programme with serviced sites and factory units, and small grants, rent guarantees and commercial advice to small firms. But it had limited resources and could not address the demand deficiency in the local economy. It created less than 2,000 jobs at a time when tens of thousands of jobs were being lost in the city. At the same time the private sector did not help and failed to construct relationships with the local authority. They were either contributing to the problem by retrenching and creating unemployment or they were desperately trying to protect their existing businesses. During Liverpool's lost decade its economic failure was compounded by leadership failure.[9]

The radicalisation of Labour – municipal socialism and confrontation

The peculiarities of Liverpool politics, which were different from other UK cities, contributed to the city's crisis. For complex social reasons, Liverpool was governed for much of the twentieth century not by Labour but by the Conservative Party. The Labour Party had never had a grip upon Liverpool's voters. Despite its working-class structure and proletarian culture, the city was never a Labour stronghold. A tradition of casualism and sectarianism within the working classes based on historic Irish immigration prevented Labour from taking control in Liverpool until 1955 – thirty years after it had captured many other big cities. The Conservative Party, by winning the votes of working-class Protestants, controlled Liverpool for over a century. Even after it won control in the mid-1950s, Labour had to share power with the Conservatives. In the 1970s this pattern was shattered by the emergence of the Liberal Party.

The economic and political failures of the 1970s sowed the seeds for an even more traumatic political crisis in the city when Labour took control in the 1980s. During the 1970s two important realignments had taken place in Liverpool. First, the Labour Party gradually moved from being a minority party to achieving the political dominance that the city's class structure suggested it should have. The Liberal Party seized control of the city government at the beginning of the 1970s, but it actually lost ground to Labour throughout the decade, only preventing Labour from coming to power by squeezing the Conservative Party out of the city. During the 1970s the classic Liverpool politics of religion and sectarianism were replaced by the politics of class, as the Conservative Party inexorably lost its grip on working-class Protestant voters. By the beginning of the 1980s Labour was poised to construct the one-party state that dominated other provincial industrial cities in Britain. At the end of the decade this had become a reality.

The second realignment in the city was that as the Liverpool electorate slowly turned to Labour, the local party itself was moving from its traditional right-of-centre ground to the far left. Indeed, during the late 1970s the party came under the control of the Militant Tendency, a Trotskyist faction that, although a minority in the party, exploited its organisational superiority to take control of the party and shape its policies. As the manufacturing unions declined and the local-authority-employed white- and blue-collar unions became more important in the Labour Party, they pushed it towards conflict with the Conservative government. This was exploited by Militant, which was using Liverpool to conduct a wider national struggle with the Conservative government.[10] It persuaded the Liverpool Labour Party that it should threaten to bankrupt the city when it gained control unless government gave the city more resources for public services.[11] And Liverpool voters voted for the strategy.[12] This was encouraged by a leading Militant Tendency member, Derek Hatton, a flamboyant orator but a controversial figure. He was the deputy leader of the Labour group on the city council, but its de facto leader. He made the running in the confrontation.

So in 1983, when Labour won the first absolute majority on Liverpool City Council for over a decade, the city's financial affairs stopped being a technical issue and became instead a highly charged political event. Labour's victory ended the political uncertainty and lack of leadership. But the period of decisive leadership brought a new set of problems for the city. Labour was committed to reversing the policies of its Liberal predecessors. In particular, Labour had become increasingly frustrated with the Liberals' use of public funds to encourage the private sector while reducing support for public housing. In Labour's view the public sector had to be the engine of economic growth in a depressed city and maximum resources should be committed to preserving public-sector employment and rehabilitating and expanding the public housing stock in the most deprived areas of the city. Labour's fiscal argument with government was complex but it had a simple message. The local authority, with 31,000 employees, was the largest employer in a city that had unemployment over 20%. Government cuts to the city's revenue and capital budgets were further depressing the city's economy and creating fiscal stress for the council. In fact many of the city council officers at the time agreed about the unfairness of the city's treatment by government. Ever since 1978 senior officers had gone to Whitehall to present their concerns about the broader impact of public expenditure cuts on the city, and more specifically the effects of the new grant regime on the city council's fiscal position. But every year the government thanked its visitors and reassured them, in the words of the chief executive at the time, Alfred Stocks, that they would 'bear it in mind for next year Alfred'. But they never did.

Labour's strategy encountered two major objections at the time. One was that employment in the local authority or investment in public housing was essentially investment in consumption, which did little to create long-term economic development. A more powerful argument was that, regardless of whether the strategy was desirable, it was not possible since it could not be funded. The Conservative government elected in 1979 was determined to limit the growth of the public sector and specifically was restricting revenue and capital expenditure by local authorities. This meant that Liverpool could not expand its workforce or sustain a major house-building programme. However, Labour

Labour
councillors
march
© Dave Sinclair

argued that it had an electoral mandate to resist the government's policy and to use any political or financial tactics to sustain the level of economic demand in the city. From 1983 until 1987 the argument became increasingly vitriolic and dominated the national headlines. In 1984, after a bitter confrontation with the government and threats by the Labour council to bankrupt the city, the government allocated marginal extra funding to the council to ease its fiscal problems. However, political exploitation of the victory by the Militant Tendency and Derek Hatton in particular convinced the Conservative government that it was pointless trying to help the city. Militant, which had ambitions to play on a broader national stage, used it as an important platform for its recruitment campaign across the country. Hatton claimed to have given Thatcher a bloody nose and that Liverpool was a perfect advert for what a hard left party could do if it stood up to government. Hatton argued. 'There is no way Thatcher can take on the might of the working class in this city. And this is just the start.'[13] Patrick Jenkin, the Minister for Local Government at the time, accused him of trying 'to dance on my grave'. He argued, 'They can't expect us to put up with this forever. It is increasingly difficult for me to sell the need for substantial additional help for Liverpool when all they do is to turn around and kick us in the teeth. People ask, "Why are you wasting your time and our money on an unappreciative part of the country?"'[14] Thatcher had taken it equally personally, claiming that 'they do not have respect for my office … these people must be put down'.[15]

Labour refused either to cut its services or its employees or to increase the rates to pay for them. Instead it insisted that the government had a moral obligation to fund the council's revenue deficit. But each year the government refused to help, and the council balanced its books in a technically legitimate but financially imprudent way by transferring resources from its capital programme to its revenue programme to pay part of its employees' salaries. In 1985 Labour eventually abandoned its threat after elaborate creative accounting. But it delayed setting its rate until several months into the financial year when the city was on the brink of bankruptcy. In 1986 the Labour council did set a rate on time but fixed its expenditure at £37 million higher than its income, arguing that the government owed it that much money. For several months Liverpool again hovered on the brink of financial collapse until a major bank loan in July allowed further creative accounting and the temporary postponement of the fiscal crisis for another year.[16]

Did Labour actually have an economic plan for the city – as opposed to just confrontation?

Labour was arguing with the Conservative government's grant allocation because it insisted that it prevented the council from taking steps to tackle the city's underlying economic and social problems. Behind the public confrontation over money, Labour was trying to reform the council. It was beginning to

1980s council
billboard
© Dave Sinclair

reorganise secondary schools; rationalise further education; reorganise housing management and rationalise refuse collection. But its primary effort to regenerate Liverpool's economy was its Urban Regeneration Strategy. Despite the scope of the title, the programme was relatively limited. Essentially it consisted of a public housing programme with some environmental improvements and leisure facilities. Little attention was paid to other elements of an economic development strategy. The growing potential of the city centre as a retail, leisure and tourism site was ignored, as were the cultural industries. Equally little effort was paid to supply-side measures such as training, the supply of capital, enterprise development or the development of SMEs. But in its own terms the strategy had a major impact on the city's physical environment. It built 4,000 new homes and refurbished 8,000 existing ones, built five leisure centres and created three new public parks. Most of the city's late Victorian or 1960s slums were demolished or substantially modernised. However, it focused on only a few parts of the city, and other areas continued to deteriorate. Capital expenditure predominated, with little money for maintenance. The council made little progress in improving the quality of its own workforce, which meant that many tenants received poor maintenance service, undermining much of the value of the new house-building programme.

More important in leadership terms, Labour's strategy alienated much of the private sector in the city. Major developers and construction interests approved of the programme, which provided them with a lot of work. But other commercial, retail and industrial firms found the concentration of money almost entirely in the council's working-class heartland, and the dogmatic way in which it was being driven through the city, alien. By 1986 relations between Labour politicians and the business class in Liverpool were at a nadir, with huge cultural and ideological differences between them. The Militant leadership, which was driving the strategy, although a minority in the party, had a powerful organisational grip on it. This was reinforced by the fact that the Labour Party was dominated by blue-collar unions, many of whose members were council employees and feared losing their jobs if the council adopted a more conciliatory strategy. By this time an enormously powerful Labour politician, Tony Byrne, who was not in fact a Militant but a calculating and clever Leftist determined to protect Liverpool from Thatcher's Toryism, had emerged to control both the city's financial affairs and its regeneration strategy. He refused to make any concessions on the strategy to internal or external critics. His dominance emphasised another aspect of the weakness of leadership in the city. The Labour Party, with its workerist ideology and style and its cultural disdain for middle-class elements, produced very few alternative leaders who had the political or administrative experience to generate a different strategy around which internal critics in the party could mobilise.

Leadership and a culture of failure

'It was a strange time. There was huge political energy. But amongst the officers there was a sense of fatalism and the need to keep their heads down.'
– John Flamson, former chief planner, Merseyside Development Corporation

There was a cultural dimension to this pattern of failure. The secular decline of the economy, the rapid emigration of many qualified residents, the political paralysis of the 1970s and the divisions of the 1980s, and the failure of so many government initiatives had an important effect upon the city's local economic and political elites. It had created a failure of confidence and an inability to mobilise existing social capital around the city's objectively powerful case. The tactical disasters of the Labour council in its budget crises were *sui generis*. But the self-destructive behaviour of the time found an echo in civic life in Liverpool. Economic change requires constructive political responses. But Liverpool was a house divided. Its leadership rarely reached the heights necessary to face demoralising decline. The public and private sectors were both weak and political relations between them had been strained. Liverpool's relationship with central government was controversial and it had attracted little national goodwill or money.

The city's social structure was dominated by a large working class and its culture. Its middle class was relatively small. Class relations mediated through political parties and trade union action were tense. The education and skill levels of the community were relatively low. There had been consistent emigration and little immigration to produce dynamic new social groups. The city lacked an entrepreneurial tradition. The city council had become a demoralised and inefficient organisation that had lacked clear political or administrative leadership for over a decade. The absence of indigenous capital and the branch plant syndrome also drained local leadership. The private sector had produced few powerful leaders willing to commit their personal or corporate resources to civic life. It was no accident that Liverpool's most powerful advocates during this period were neither politicians nor business leaders but the two Church leaders – Bishop David Sheppard and Archbishop Derek Worlock. They tried to mobilise local elites, to talk to government and represent the wider interest of the city. And they were at least listened to by government – even if they did not necessarily shift the thrust of government policy.[17]

No support for or votes in the city centre

The highly partisan nature of the political debate during the 1970s and 1980s meant that it was dominated by short-term electoral imperatives and competition for votes over two issues – the level of local taxation and the scope and future of public housing in the city. By focusing attention and resources on working-class residential areas on the periphery of the city, these priorities prevented the potential role of the city centre as a driver of economic development getting on to the political agenda. There was little political mileage in it and little attention was paid to it. These political preferences were complemented by those of the planners. Throughout much of the period professional planning was in favour of slum clearance, decanting people to peripheral areas and minimising traffic congestion in city centres. Liverpool was no exception. These political and administrative attitudes prevented the city council from developing a clear vision of the city centre in terms of generating jobs and wealth and enhancing the local quality of life. The ideological character of the Liverpool Labour Party contributed to this failure. The party was dominated by working-class interests and by blue-collar rather than by skilled craft unions. This not only gave the party a particular leadership structure and policies that were primarily oriented towards the needs of its working-class supporters and members. It also affected the party's internal political culture, which became dogmatic, exclusive and workerist in tone. This meant that the party was primarily interested in issues around production and particularly with jobs for manual workers. The economic potential of activities such as tourism, leisure, the arts and culture, retail or even white-collar service-sector jobs which were concentrated in the city centre was regarded with scepticism.

A weak private sector

These Labour party priorities also opened a major cultural gap with the private sector in the city. It was felt that Labour was hostile to business interests. This underlined another feature of Liverpool during this period – the limited contribution that the private sector made to the city's economic and civic life. This was explained by a variety of factors. Most obvious was the fact that the decline of the private sector of the economy during the recession of the 1970s meant that the city's largest economic actors were primarily in the public sector. The city council, the health services, the university and polytechnic were the largest employers and biggest players. Equally important was that many of the private-sector interests were large employers, often national and multinational corporations which did not regard themselves primarily as local firms with a direct stake in the local economy. The dominance of large firms meant that Liverpool had little in the way of a tradition of small firms that could provide local leadership. The massive loss of middle-class population from the region and the suburbanisation of many professionals who worked in but lived outside the city's boundaries also meant that the pool of leaders who were committed to the city and who might promote the city centre as an alternative focus for economic development remained small.

Government, Liverpool and special urban initiatives

This mood of local chauvinism and the confrontation with government was encouraged by the city's experience of central government's urban strategy over twenty years. Liverpool since the 1960s had been the target of every initiative, including Educational Priority Areas, the Urban Programme, General Improvement Areas, Community Development Projects, Inner Area Studies, Enterprise Zones and Inner City Partnerships. But however well-intentioned, these had not made a major dent in Liverpool's economic problems and hence increased local scepticism about what could be achieved with special government initiatives. In part the analysis was wrong. In part there was not enough money. In part different government departments did not work together well enough. They were ad hoc and divorced from many mainstream programmes. They stopped and started without much rationale.[18] This had led many politicians and even administrators to question whether government was serious or cared enough about the city. This partly applied to Labour governments. But the Thatcher government's commitment to roll back the state and replace it with private-sector-led regeneration was the straw that broke the camel's back for many in Liverpool – politicians, local government officers and voters. As the government began to cut public expenditure and support for the city along the way, the belief grew that Liverpool had no place in the Conservative government's view of the world and that it was redundant politically and economically. By the early 1980s the government reciprocated these feelings. It saw Liverpool as expensive, inefficient, badly run and incapable of responding adequately politically or administratively to the problems it faced.

There was only one real exception to this Tory view of Liverpool then and now – Michael Heseltine. Heseltine got, spoke for and lobbied for Liverpool, at a time when few other national – certainly Tory – politicians could or would. Nearly all of the crucial initiatives and projects discussed in this book had his fingerprints on them. He was Minister for Merseyside after the Toxteth riots and persuaded a sceptical Thatcher government to stick with rather than give up on Liverpool. He

invented Urban Development Corporations which put Albert Dock at the centre of the city's renaissance. He invented the Merseyside Special Allocation, which many years before its time adopted the non-departmental, place-based approach to urban problems that is currently fashionable. He invented City Challenge, which was another crucial part of Liverpool's renaissance jigsaw. Heseltine was also influential in making sure that Merseyside was given the European Commission's Objective 1 status in 1994, which was the driver of so much of this change. He started the clean-up of the polluted River Mersey which at the time he called 'an open sewer'. He wrote an influential report on the future of the city region's economy with Sir Terry Leahy in 2011. He promoted the idea of elected mayors and city regions which became an important part of Liverpool's more successful governance in recent years. But he was a lone beacon for Liverpool in the Conservative Party – certainly then and probably now.

Getting off the brink – Labour's internal revolution

During the mid-1980s the political and economic life of Liverpool was in turmoil. There seemed no obvious way of breaking the impasse, since Labour was consistently returned to office with an apparently popular mandate for its policies and tactics. The government could never understand why Liverpool's voters kept supporting the confrontation and bankruptcy strategy. It seemed like self-destructive financial suicide. The answer was that they were protesting to government. More than just Labour voters were opposed to government policies, and even some of its own supporters in the city had doubts. Popular understanding of technical budget issues was slight and people seemed confused about what was going to happen. But the voters had grasped the main outlines of the story and connected it with the picture of obvious economic, physical and social decline they could witness daily around them. The private sector was collapsing and unemployment was rising and lasting longer. However tangentially related, crime and drug abuse were also seen to be on the increase. Under these circumstances, the government's policy of cutting public expenditure and reducing the money spent on housing and local authority jobs seemed to lack common sense. Local chauvinism as much as ideology underpinned their resentment of Thatcher's government's apparent lack of concern for the city. As one voter put it to a Liberal Party canvasser, 'I can't stand the Militant. But at least someone is standing up to the Bitch in London.'

But the Labour council overplayed its hand and the campaign against the government and its national party leadership eventually failed and led to its own downfall. In 1985 the national Labour Party leadership, worried about the impact of the Liverpool crisis on its national reputation, suspended the Liverpool city party, and in 1986 it expelled several leading party members for their membership of the proscribed Militant Tendency and for abuse of party

Liverpool against the Militants demonstration
© Dave Sinclair

rules during the budget campaign against the government. In 1985 47 Labour councillors were surcharged and disqualified from office by the District Auditor. In 1987 the House of Lords confirmed the District Auditor's initial judgement that the council had failed to protect the city's financial interests and expelled 47 councillors from office. Until the Labour council was disqualified from office, it managed to sustain its programme by borrowing almost £60 million from foreign banks, which would be repaid in later years. But as government tightened its rules on such schemes throughout the decade, the pressures on the council simply grew. By the end of the decade a new, more moderate Labour council was forced increasingly into desperate financial remedies just to sustain its revenue and capital programme and balance its books.

The subsequent reorganisation of the Labour Party by the national leadership and the elections to replace the disqualified councillors provided the opportunity for other groups to emerge in leadership positions in the party, and for other policies to be followed. In fact despite the expulsions and disqualifications, Labour was returned to power with an even greater majority. But as a result of considerable internal manoeuvring during the recruitment and selection process, the majority of the new councillors were closer to the political centre or at least opposed to the tactics if not necessarily the policies of the Militant Tendency. During its first year in office a new party leader emerged, who had previously led Merseyside County Council, Keva Coombes. He was a lawyer with considerable political experience, who had the ability to balance the ideological interests in the party and reassure the local private sector that the policies of confrontation with them and with the government would be abandoned. Such Labour guarantees of moderation were virtually inevitable. It had become clear to all sectors that the politics of confrontation had not only failed to extract extra resources for the city, but had also lost it local and national allies. Equally it was becoming difficult for Labour to sustain its predecessor's massive capital works programme, since between 1983 and 1987 the programme had anticipated and consumed future resources, leaving the new council to cope with the financial consequences. So the new group could not afford the policies of the old Labour group, even if it had wanted to.

Although a substantial minority of both the Labour Party and the newly elected council remained members of the Militant Tendency or supported its policies, the new Labour leadership spent the next few years trying to find a way of staying faithful to the goal of municipal employment and building public housing while finding an accommodation with the local private sector, potential investors and government. This leadership attempted to develop a new economic strategy for the city through a tentative series of initiatives and alliances in which the city centre began to play an important part. As the council increasingly recognised the potential of the area, it spent considerable time attempting to develop a public–private partnership between itself and other key local actors – the Merseyside Development Corporation, the government's Merseyside Task Force and local business interests. This for the first time focused on the need to renovate, develop and market the city centre as the heart of a campaign to improve Liverpool's image and attract external inward investment.

Rethinking Liverpool's economic future – and the city centre

The condition of the city centre was an important issue at this time because the standard of general environmental maintenance by the city council was relatively poor. The decade of paralysis and the later confrontations of the 1970s and 1980s had created tensions and conflicts between the municipal blue-collar workers and Labour politicians on the one hand, and city council managers on the other, which had led to a dramatic decline in the efficiency of the council's manual workers. The tight links between the manual workforce, their trade unions and the power structure in the Liverpool Labour Party meant that for over a decade inefficient and antiquated work practices could not be confronted or eliminated by management. As a result standards of maintenance were low throughout the city and especially bad in the city centre. Even though the architectural fabric of much of the central commercial and retail quarters was basically good, their routine appearance was not compatible with the city's ambitions to develop and market Liverpool as a tourist destination and a vibrant dynamic creative city. To make things worse, the links between blue-collar unions and the Labour council which allowed low-quality street traders in the most prestigious shopping areas only reinforced the image of Liverpool as a downmarket, low-status shopping area.

Labour's strategy generated new priorities – focusing upon the new consumption-oriented as opposed to the traditional production-oriented sectors of the city's economy.[19] In part the new Labour leadership saw the city centre in a different way from its predecessors, recognising the many opportunities that had not been and could be exploited. Whereas the previous Labour administration had concentrated resources on municipal services in the city's most deprived areas, the new strategy emphasised the potential of the city centre in terms of retail, culture, tourism, leisure and commercial development. In the late 1980s a steady stream of strategy documents emerged about the arts and cultural industries and tourism, advocating the need to diversify the economic base of the city and in particular to regenerate the city centre.

This shift partly reflected the fact that the city did not have the money to pay for a big housing programme. It also reflected the realisation that although the city council could exercise only limited leverage over the operation of the private market, it did have control over the city centre environment, which provided more than 40% of the jobs in the city. The new Labour group's view of the potential of the city centre was shaped by less overtly political factors. A crucial one was the achievements of the Merseyside Development Corporation's focus on the potential of tourism, leisure and heritage in Liverpool. The MDC had been set up by Michael Heseltine to lead the regeneration of Liverpool's docklands. Separate from the city council and endowed with substantial government resources and planning powers, the MDC gradually developed a tourism- and leisure-led strategy that had begun to bear fruit. By the end of the 1980s it had made substantial progress in physically renovating the docks on the city's waterfront and was beginning to serve as a focus for a growing tourism and leisure sector, as we shall see later. These developments had not only transformed parts of the physical core of the city. They had placed on the agenda the issue of Liverpool's potential in the tourism and leisure industries and of the relationship between the waterfront and the adjacent city centre. They forced the city council to focus on the regeneration potential of culture, leisure and the city centre. During the Militant period the council had seen the MDC as a Whitehall-imposed institution that had diverted government resources from the local authority, and had refused to collaborate with it. The emergence of the new moderate group in 1987 allowed peace to break out and a dialogue about common interests emerged.

But despite the council's changing priorities, one problem was that the proposals required resources and cooperation between a range of sectors over which it did not have control. The council was essentially setting the agenda for the regeneration of the city without necessarily being able to generate the financial, administrative and human resources needed to deliver it. It did make changes where it could, using the limited Urban Programme money of £20 million to move away from housing to pedestrianising substantial parts of the city centre, creating a park to link the city centre to the waterfront and paying for the refurbishment of the city's theatres. The money was also used to encourage small business to hire apprentices, to develop a security scheme on inner-city sites and provide incentives to potential external investors. The council commissioned a variety of consultancy studies to examine the tourist potential of the city, the problem of the city's image and city marketing, the economic potential of the design industry and most significantly the merits of creating in the city a public–private partnership to guide economic development. Their significance was that the initiatives reflected the priorities of the Conservative government's urban strategy and many of them actively involved the participation of business groups such as the Chamber of Commerce, the Stores Committee as well as the MDC. Essentially the council used its limited resources to send a signal to government, the local private sector and potential investors that the era of confrontation was over and the council recognised the need to work in partnership with them.

Liverpool off the brink ...

At the end of the 1980s Liverpool appeared to be at a turning point. The economic collapse of the early 1980s had been arrested. There was some growth taking place in modern sectors of the economy. The political complexion of the city had changed and many of the internal divisions of the past seemed reduced.

Cooperation rather than conflict characterised relations between the city council, the private sector, the MDC and government officials – if not always politicians. There was some agreement among many of the major institutions about which sectors of the economy had development potential and should be exploited. There was recognition among elites of the problems that had been created by the recent political confusion and conflicts for potential investment in the city. There was a clearer view of where it wished to go and a willingness on the part of the public and private sectors to collaborate to promote the city's long-term interests. The conflicts of the 1980s had been replaced with greater consensus about the agenda for the 1990s.

In the real economy progress had also been made in the cultural industries sector. The efforts of the MDC were beginning to show fruit.[20] Tourism was expanding and the waterfront was substantially improved. The city council had recognised the crucial importance of the city centre as a focus for economic development and accepted the need to manage and maintain it better to integrate it into the developing tourist quarter waterfront. The manufacturing sector had shed jobs but become more efficient. The service sector was picking up some momentum. The residential market was improving. Wavertree Technology Park had been created. The port had become efficient and profitable even though its workforce had declined from 40,000 to 3,000. And office building in the city centre was beginning to happen. The city centre had experienced considerable physical refurbishment of its public and private spaces during the latter part of the decade.

... but not out of the woods

But a series of economic challenges remained. Unemployment was still 16% and poverty was experienced in some form by 50% of the population. The economic recovery of the city was fragile and remained vulnerable to downturns in the national or regional economy. The economic growth that had occurred was uneven, concentrated in particular sectors of the economy and areas of the city. Substantial unemployment and physical dereliction in many parts of the city posed continuing economic and potential political problems.[21] This raised issues about the potential level of demand for consumption services and whether greater effort should be made in the production industries. In particular a cultural policy that would focus on the city as a centre for tourism and retailing – sectors typically characterised by low skills, low pay and poor levels of job satisfaction – would need to be balanced by job creation strategies in more highly skilled, high-value-added sectors such as design, electronic music, film and broadcasting. Also a focus on city centre jobs would have to be set against increasing opportunities for people living in deprived outer estates and inner-city communities.

There were also significant political challenges. There had been a change of mood in the city about its economic future. But at that point Liverpool had not yet clearly demonstrated that it had the political leadership, administrative capacity, financial resources or public commitment needed to turn policy intentions into genuine achievements. There were significant constraints on the council. It remained unreconstructed. The quality of its services declined during the 1970s and 1980s. It had difficulties recruiting top people and its political culture was divided and negative. In 1988 the chief executive resigned because of his inability to move the administrative machinery, and the city could not attract a new chief executive for over a year. And although the council had abandoned the high-profile confrontation with government, its financial position was very challenging. The ruling Labour group remained divided about policy and its left-wing leadership was suspended in 1990 by the national Labour Party leadership. So clear political leadership and stability had not been achieved.

More widely, Liverpool had not yet generated a clear strategy for economic development and an internal consensus about the nature of the strategy that should be used and the means of achieving it, although one was beginning to emerge. A partnership between the public and private sectors had been created which was attempting to develop a long-term marketing strategy. Relations between the city council and central government had clearly improved since the Militant era. There were many innovative projects planned, but they did not form a clear strategy that linked priorities and resources to agreed goals and actions. And the city had an image problem. Its image of industrial and political militancy, though not necessarily accurate, meant that the city would need a long-term campaign to redress the problem. There was also an internal image problem. Two decades of failure had bred a degree of cynicism in the city's public life. There was a cultural dimension to the city's failure that went beyond the statistics of economic decline.

Liverpool needed to undergo structural economic and social modernisation to cope with the decade beyond the 1980s. In terms of institutions, a bankrupt local authority could make some contribution, but it did not have the powers and resources necessary for the task. The MDC had too narrow a geographical remit and was too unaccountable to do the job in the long term. Arguably the city needed to boost short-term employment; upgrade the physical environment; upgrade its existing social capital to meet the needs of future markets and the private sector; create a strategy for both sunrise and sunset industries and generate the investment to implement it. The evidence was that although a programme was necessary it would not be quick, and it would need sustained underpinning by the public sector. I argued at the time that the private sector on its own would not do it, the local authority could not do it and central government was too distant. The alternative of continued drift was ominous. The experience of successful cities in coming to terms with decline was that if economic confidence was to be restored, the public sector would have to play a key role. In fact this turned out subsequently to be true.

But the public money involved was not the UK government's but the European Commission's.[22]

At the end of the 1980s urban entrepreneurialism had replaced municipal socialism in the UK as the preferred strategy of many city leaders. The experience of a number of cities indicated that the path was having some success. It suggested that the policies and actions of leaders could affect the development path of the city. It at least suggested that positive action was preferable to blind acquiescence in the face of economic change, even if one could not control it. Liverpool was beginning to go down that path. But its range of structural economic, environmental, political and cultural problems suggested that the city would remain one of the most testing cases for urban regeneration. Its experience had demonstrated that political failure could exaggerate economic failure. The question for the 1990s was could good political leadership be generated and would it encourage economic success?[23]

Notes

1   Michael Parkinson, 'Leadership and Regeneration in Liverpool: Confusion, Conflict or Coalition?', in Judd and Parkinson (eds), *Leadership and Urban Regeneration*.

2   Richard Meegan, 'Urban Regeneration, Policies and Social Cohesion: The Liverpool Case', in Munck (ed.), *Reinventing the City*; Stuart Wilks Heeg, 'From World City to Pariah City? Liverpool and the Global Economy 1850–2000', in Munck (ed.), *Reinventing the City*; Richard Meegan, 'Paradise Postponed', in Philip Cooke (ed.), *Localities* (Unwin Hyman, 1988).

3   Parkinson, *Liverpool on the Brink*, p. 12.

4   Quoted in Parkinson, *Liverpool on the Brink*, p. 15.

5   Michael Heseltine, *Life in the Jungle: An Autobiography* (Hodder and Stoughton, 2003).

6   Michael Parkinson and James Duffy, 'Government Response to Inner City Riots: The Minister for Merseyside and Task Force', *Parliamentary Affairs*, 37.1 (1984).

7   Heseltine, *Life in the Jungle: An Autobiography*, p. 217.

8   Michael Parkinson, 'Liverpool's Real Crisis', *New Society*, 11 October 1985.

9   Parkinson, 'Leadership and Regeneration in Liverpool'.

10   Peter Taaffe and Tony Mulhearn, *Liverpool: The City that Dared to Fight* (Fortress Books, 1988); Derek Hatton, *Inside Left: The Story So Far* (Bloomsbury, 1988); Militant, *Liverpool Fights the Tories* (Militant Publications, 1984).

11   Michael Parkinson, 'Why New York is Liverpool's Shining Example', *The Guardian*, 2 April 1984.

12   Michael Parkinson, 'Mandate for a City of Strife', *The Guardian*, 30 May 1984.

13   Parkinson, *Liverpool on the Brink*, p. 108.

14   Parkinson, *Liverpool on the Brink*, p. 126.

15   Quoted in Parkinson, *Liverpool on the Brink*, p. 148.

16   Michael Parkinson, 'Liverpool's Fiscal Crisis: An Anatomy of Failure', in Parkinson, Foley and Judd (eds), *Regenerating the Cities*; Michael Parkinson, 'Fiscal Stress in Britain: The Liverpool Experience', in Terry Nichols Clark et al. (eds), *Research in Urban Policy*, 3 (JAI Press, 1989); Michael Parkinson, 'Big Cities and Fiscal Stress', in S. Villadsen (ed.), *Big City Politics: Problems and Strategies* (Copenhagen, 1990); Michael Parkinson, 'Officer's Dilemma', *Public Money*, 1 (1987); Michael Parkinson, 'Creative Accounting and Financial Ingenuity in Local Government', *Public Money*, 4 (1986).

17   David Sheppard and Derek Worlock, *Better Together* (Hodder and Stoughton, 1988); Michael Parkinson, 'God's Biased Umpires', *New Society*, 22 January 1988.

18   Michael Parkinson, 'Twenty-Five Years of Urban Policy in Britain – Partnership, Entrepreneurialism or Competition?', *Public Money & Management* (1996).

19   Michael Parkinson, 'Liverpool: A Tale of Missed Opportunities', in Bianchini and Parkinson (eds), *Cultural Policy and Urban Regeneration*.

20   Michael Parkinson, 'On Liverpool's Waterfront', *New Society*, 14 June 1986.

21   Michael Parkinson, 'Requalification urbaine et développement inégal dans une ville traditionnelle', in *Les Villes Européennes de Traditionnel Industrielle* (Presses Universitaires de Lille, 1994); Michael Parkinson, 'Port-City Lifestyles: Liverpool', in *Vivre et Habiter la Ville Portuaire* (Paris, 1994).

22   Parkinson, 'Leadership and Regeneration in Liverpool', p. 256.

23   Michael Parkinson and Hilary Russell, *Economic Attractiveness and Social Exclusion: The Case of Liverpool* (European Institute for Urban Affairs, report to the European Commission, 2004).

CHAPTER THREE

Liverpool begins to become normal, 1988–98

The 1990s were a crucial bridge between the confusion and chaos of the 1980s and the European ambitions of the 2000s. Several key features marked the period. First, the Liverpool Labour Party moved further away from the Militant legacy towards the political centre as it tried to distance itself from the bad old days, although there remained two wings within the party. Secondly, there was a significant effort to deal with the weaknesses of the local authority – even though this was not wholly successful. Thirdly, there was a growing recognition of the need for partnership working between the public and private sectors, which was encouraged by both national government and the European Commission. Fourthly, there was a growing recognition, encouraged by Europe, of the importance of scale and the need for Liverpool to work at the wider city region level. Finally and most significantly, there was a growing recognition of the importance of the city centre economy to the future of Liverpool and increased efforts to improve its performance.

Putting Humpty Dumpty together again – four big city initiatives

A key feature of the Liverpool renaissance story is how the economic, physical and social disintegration of the city was gradually tackled, if not resolved, in the 1990s and 2000s. Slowly during this period the different parts of the city, which had lost their economic rationale and had been fragmented by the loss of population during the 1970s and 1980s, were gradually tied together into a more coherent place physically.[1] During the 1990s the city's political, administrative

Albert Dock,
Liverpool
© Ken Biggs/Alamy
Stock Photo

and business leadership began to recognise the need to regenerate the declining city centre. Given the scale of collapse in the manufacturing and port sectors, the potential of business, professional, financial, retail, and tourism and knowledge sectors was an obvious – but previously neglected – area to exploit. This growing awareness can best be illustrated by four major initiatives that helped to transform the debate about Liverpool's economy and to significantly improve the performance of the city centre in particular. They were Liverpool City Challenge, the Merseyside Development Corporation, Speke Garston Development Company and Regeneration Partnership, and the European Commission's Objective 1 Programme. They were the keys to the successes of the 1990s.

The Merseyside Development Corporation operated on the Liverpool waterfront and began its work in the early 1980s, as we saw in the previous chapter. It had important successes then, but much of its impact was felt during the 1990s. Liverpool City Challenge was a five-year government-funded programme at the edge of Liverpool city centre which ran from 1992 to 1997. The Speke Garston project from 1996 to 2004 also had government money to tackle different economic and social challenges in a declining industrial area where the airport, the Ford motor company and many pharmaceutical companies were based in the otherwise relatively comfortable suburban south Liverpool. An even more significant contribution was made by the European Objective 1 Programme which between 1994 and 2006 invested £1.5 billion in infrastructure, skills and neighbourhood capacity building across the whole of the city region.

These projects were typical of the regeneration initiatives of the time. All were area-based projects with guaranteed resources and teams to deliver, and a partnership board to govern them. All were externally proposed and funded rather than internally generated. The first two were introduced by national government and in both cases by the same person – Michael Heseltine. They directly and indirectly encouraged partnership working. But they were also the primary sources of external investment as local authorities themselves remained financially squeezed and reliant increasingly on ad hoc national and European government intervention. Some of the initiatives formally either began or ended after the 1990s such as the MDC and Objective 1. But their impact was particularly felt during this decade. They demonstrated different ways of addressing economic and urban decline. They helped change the institutional governance framework and political culture of Liverpool. They helped lay the foundations for future economic development. They all helped to start making Liverpool's politics normal.

Political and administrative normalisation first

However, these externally generated initiatives could not have worked if the city's leadership, especially the city council, was not willing to change its attitudes and behaviour. The initiatives required a different relationship with government and with the private sector, as well as a different level of performance from the local authority, which was to be a key player in the regeneration process during the 1990s. An important political change happened in 1990 when the Labour Party elected the former deputy leader of Merseyside County Council, Harry Rimmer, to lead the council group and replace the existing leader Keva Coombes, who had been allied with the broad left of the party. This election of the centre-right leader took place after a bitter debate in which the broad left walked out. An old-fashioned municipal leader who had been prominent in Merseyside County Council before it was abolished by Thatcher, Rimmer was a key figure in moving from the confrontational to the 'responsible' model of politics in Liverpool. He got government to change its view about Liverpool as a place where it was possible to do business. In fact, Rimmer was so adept at charming the Tories that the legendary quote from the Tory minister was 'that man has cost me millions'. Rimmer also led the charge to get European Objective 1 funding and pressed the city's case with European leaders, getting Michael Heseltine to support the case behind closed doors. He provided a crucial bridge from the politics of confrontation to the politics of realism.

Although the Labour group remained divided, Rimmer's election publicly demonstrated the council's commitment to mainstream politics and policies and a new era of economic regeneration. Liverpool, he said, needed 'a fundamental shift. We had the worst services anywhere in the UK. It was the costliest but in terms of what people got its performance was abysmal. We were grossly overstaffed. Liverpool needs to rise to its challenge and become more efficient and come to terms with the realities of the modern world and modern life.'[2] He had three priorities when he took office. First, the city council had to improve its image and show it was 'better than the last lot'. Secondly, it had to win friends in high places and develop better connections with senior decision makers in government, public agencies and the private sector. Thirdly, it had to adopt a Liverpool stands alone mentality – the city would have to become competitive and win and deliver projects. It led to some wins, with the city getting significant government programmes and resources.

Rimmer's leadership led to some important administrative stability as well. When he took power there had not been a chief executive in the city for almost two years. Rimmer soon appointed a new chief executive, Peter Bounds, giving him the challenge 'For goodness sake Peter, make the place normal.' Bounds was an old-school local government chief executive who was right for the place at the time. He had done a good job fixing the town centre in Bolton. He knew he could run a big city local authority. He had been passing through the city and went down Lime Street and saw that all the streetlights were out. He asked himself who would come and sort this out. His answer was someone who had done the job before and who knew how to run an urban authority. So he applied and got the job. Others agreed he was the right the man for the time. Proper, respectable, wise and emollient were typical adjectives applied to him.

Bounds did not make as much progress as he had hoped with council reform, but his thoughtful, measured, diplomatic manner helped hold Liverpool together at a very difficult time when it could have gone into further political decline. He encouraged partnerships and was willing to let the city council give up control of many things. This approach was perfectly illustrated by his supporting and chairing of both Liverpool City Challenge and Speke Garston Regeneration Partnership. He knew that the local authority when he took it over was 'organisationally derelict' and needed to improve. But he also knew that government policy was a ragbag of initiatives that made it very difficult to manage a city coherently. He established the principle that the local authority's real purpose was to deliver decent services to local people rather than simply provide jobs for a small number of people. He was an important bridge between the chaos of the mid-1980s and the achievements of the late 1990s. Bounds himself judged that he moved the organisation and got it to a point where others later 'could do something with it'. Both Rimmer and Bounds were helped by the city council's leading thinker and strategist of those years, Alan Chape. As assistant chief executive he was crucial during the normalisation period, for example helping to raise the economic ambitions of the city council, spotting the potential of European money and recognising the city centre as a key engine of the Liverpool economy

However, making the local authority normal was a huge challenge. In Bounds's words 'the most damaging thing about all this was not the level of service itself, which was dire, but what it did to the culture of the organisation. It created a sense nothing else mattered except the preservation of jobs.'[3] They were attempting, as Chape explained, to rewire the council and to move it from 'an obsession with process and welfare to a work mentality'. They knew they had to move the agenda on to the government's ground and they made the necessary gestures to do so. As Chape again admitted, many of the things they did were essentially window dressing, because they did not have the money to put them into practice. But many were the basis of things that would come later. They put councillors on the board of the MDC, which they had resisted in the past. They tried to distance themselves as much as possible from the disqualified 47. They started lobbying government effectively, building their case and winning friends in high places. They started to build partnerships. And they started to operate more strategically. The period 1987–91 was spent fixing relationships as much as anything else. From 1991 to 1997 they started to develop a regeneration agenda and get their hands on some of the burgeoning 'funny money' available from government. They also asked the politicians 'What kind of city – not council – do you want Liverpool to be?' So politically and administratively the city was in better shape to work with government in the 1990s and to attempt to modernise the city and reshape its economy.

But the job was never easy. The politics throughout Bounds's period of office were difficult. There was a divided Labour Party, changes of party leadership and a lack of ambition by some Labour leaders. And the council was still essentially a controlling organisation, willing to give up government money rather than give up control. The city's financial position was challenging and staff cuts required by the local authority meant that it had declining capacity. In his first year Bounds had to implement deep cuts in the city council budget and there was a strike of over seven months because of 123 redundancies.[4] And the alphabet soup of government programmes, in his words, meant that 'it was no way to run a city'.[5] So he decided that the only way to run Liverpool was if someone could coordinate it – and the only body that could do that would be the city council. He saw it as his job to orchestrate the network of agencies with an interest in the city and believed he was authorised as chief executive of the city council to talk to anyone about pursuing the interests of the city. Bounds spent a lot of time trying to influence external behaviour and creating partnerships in the city as much as in the city council. There was internal dissent and those who said he spent too much time outside the council. But his view was that he should be judged as much by the changes in the city as in the city council when he finished his term of office. His two major achievements in his own eyes were that he helped 'make Liverpool respectable again' and that he captured 'the best regeneration opportunities that funny money programmes offered'. His success in changing the culture of the local authority meant that it could work with – and more importantly get funding for the city from – better-resourced public agencies in government and Europe through the MDC, City Challenge, Speke Garston and Objective 1. Better politics did bring some important rewards to the city.

Remaking Liverpool, Act 1: the Merseyside Development Corporation and the Liverpool waterfront

The first piece of the renaissance jigsaw was the work of the Merseyside Development Corporation and its efforts on the Liverpool waterfront, in particular the Albert Dock complex.[6] In fact the MDC had started its work in the early 1980s and had an important success with the opening of Tate Liverpool in Albert Dock in 1987. It was a beacon in the darkness in the city at that time. But the significance and impact of this work became particularly important in this period of normalisation. The waterfront and Albert Dock in particular was an iconic Liverpool landmark – physically, economically and politically. Ever since it was built, its fortunes had reflected those of the city itself. The completion of the dock in 1846 symbolised physically Liverpool's role as the second city of the greatest empire the world had ever known. The massive growth of the city as a global maritime force had led to a huge dock extension throughout the nineteenth century, which eventually stretched seven miles along the Mersey riverfront. Albert Dock, built by Jesse Hartley, was the first inland secure dock designed to protect its ships, goods and workers from the winds and weather of the river Mersey. The dock's fortunes flourished and declined with those of the port itself and the city. The decline and fall of the British Empire coupled with technological change and the increased size of ships posed huge economic and

Albert Dock, before redevelopment

Albert Dock, 2013
Image courtesy of Rept0n1x, Wikimedia Commons

physical challenges to Liverpool's maritime trade. The gradual decline in trade through the port after the war meant that the entire south docks, including Albert Dock, were finally made redundant in 1972. The docks north of the Pier Head continued to operate. By the 1970s Albert Dock lay derelict and abandoned, cut off by the high dock wall from the city a few hundred yards away that had been the original reason for its existence.

The whole complex could have been lost to Liverpool had it not been for the intervention of the Secretary of State for the Environment, Michael Heseltine, and his creation in 1981 of the Merseyside Development Corporation. Although it was politically and publicly controversial at the time, in Liverpool as in London, because it took control away from local authorities and put planning powers and money in the hands of nationally appointed quangos, the MDC was critical to Liverpool's physical renaissance. Its simple mission was to reclaim and regenerate the dock. It not only gave a boost to concerns with the economy of the city centre, it had the powers and resources to do something at a time when the local authority and the city had neither.

What challenges did the MDC face?

In many ways the whole enterprise was a leap of faith by the MDC, which paid off despite huge challenges at the time. Those challenges were national as well as local, and economic, physical, political and social. There was a combative Conservative government led by Margaret Thatcher during a politically troubled period. There was a recession in the 1980s with unemployment in 1981 reaching nearly 3 million. The Falklands war in 1982 was followed by the equally divisive miners' strike in 1984–85. In Liverpool itself the times were extremely challenging. The city's population collapsed from 800,000 after the war to 516,000 in 1982 and 463,000 in 1990. Employment fell from 260,000 to 217,000 between 1981 and 1989. Between 1979 and 1984 alone the city lost 44,000 manufacturing jobs. Unemployment rose from 9.2% in 1975 to 20.2% in 1981, more than double the national figure of 9.3%. The city had a dependent community of older, less skilled residents. The times were politically troubled also. There had been riots in Toxteth in 1981. The city council was controlled by the Militant Tendency between 1983 and 1987. There had been football controversies and terrible tragedies at Heysel and at Hillsborough. There were swathes of dereliction across the city. Liverpool had a poor external image. The market was depressed and investment levels were low. The city's politics were divisive and there were large conflicts and tensions between the public and private sectors. The MDC was asked to play on a sticky wicket, to say the least.

'It was the city's front door – and it was stinking and rotting.' – John Flamson

The economically redundant and physically derelict Albert Dock complex itself was a massive challenge for the MDC and the city. It developed a three-pronged strategy: the restoration of the overall water space in the south docks, the

Aerial view of
Albert Dock full
of silt, 1980
© Trinity Mirror/
Mirrorpix/Alamy
Stock Photo

redevelopment of Albert Dock itself and the International Garden Festival in 1984. The jewel in the crown was Albert Dock. MDC wanted to use its architectural and heritage assets as had been done in Boston, Baltimore and London and turn a private, run-down dockyard into a public playground and visitor destination with residential, retail, commercial and cultural facilities. The dock was intended to act as a catalyst for development in the neighbouring docklands and city centre. More widely it was hoped that it would improve the image of Liverpool, enhancing its standing as an investment location and visitor destination.

What did it achieve?

MDC's record was not unalloyed. Political instability in the city council made its task challenging. The investment market remained sluggish. It took time to shake off the poor image of Liverpool. The MDC itself remained unpopular in some parts of the city. Links between Albert Dock and the city centre remained underdeveloped. Nevertheless, the dock was in much better condition when MDC went out of business. It was always intended to be a time-limited intervention by national government, even though its boundaries and life were extended by government in 1987 to give it a bigger city centre area and more time to fix it. When it was finally closed in 1997 it had arguably achieved many, although not all, of its ambitions. It had created a historic heritage site and an attractive public realm. The Merseyside Maritime Museum was established along with Tate Liverpool and the Beatles Story. There was a programme of events and festivals around the water. There were a series of mid-market restaurants, shops, bars and cafés, and coffee shops. There was a genuine commercial offer with speciality shops, Granada Television, offices and a hotel. There were over 150 expensive river-view apartments in the Colonnades. The place had undergone significant physical, cultural and economic transformation in just over a decade.

It was a catalyst for regeneration, started quality environmental improvements, invested in underexploited sectors of the economy, and changed internal and external perceptions and the city's political standing. The International Garden Festival in 1984 had almost 3.5 million visitors and raised the profile, prestige and spirits of Liverpool and its people at a very difficult moment. The physical changes in and around Albert Dock did

Aerial view of Albert Dock, 2009
© Paul White – North West England/Alamy Stock Photo

a huge amount to raise expectations and quality standards in a city that had experienced relatively little quality development or redevelopment before the 1980s. When the MDC took over, the dock was divorced from the city centre and cut off by a major highway, the Strand. Even though more had to be done, the two had clearly been reconnected so that the waterfront seemed part of a single city. Indeed, the integration of the waterfront encouraged the building out and integration of the different zones and quarters of the city around retail, leisure, culture, business and knowledge. As Flamson argued 'the waterfront had been nationalised and democratised and had become a public rather than privatised space'.

The MDC also began initiatives in culture, housing, tourism and leisure which underlined the potential of those sectors for Liverpool's future economy. Before the 1990s tourism was not seen as real work and the economic potential of culture was undervalued. These are now acknowledged key drivers of the Liverpool city region economy. The visitor economy in particular is a major sector which employs over 54,000 people, attracts 60 million visitors and contributes over £4 billion to Liverpool's economy. The Tate Gallery, Maritime Museum and Museum of Liverpool attract 6 million visitors a year to the waterfront and Liverpool city centre. The number of city centre residents increased to over 20,000 whereas there had hardly been any before the work on the Albert Dock and the surrounding south docks.

The dock paved the way for later progress, even if it was slower than the MDC and many others had hoped. There would not have been the level of future development in the wider waterfront if Albert Dock itself had remained derelict. Image and investor confidence, which affect land values and rental levels, had been fragile. The regeneration of Albert Dock helped increase them all by doing quality work that was higher than prevailing standards in the city. It also began the process of improving partnerships between the public and private sectors in Liverpool. Most significantly, it kick-started the later renaissance of Liverpool waterfront and the wider city centre. In the 1990s and 2000s there was significant investment by the European Union in Liverpool, which underpinned major developments in the dock north of the Pier Head, south of Albert Dock with the Arena and Convention and Exhibition Centre, the renewal of the Pier Head with the completion of the Leeds–Liverpool canal, the cruise liner facility, and the Museum of Liverpool. It played a significant part in changing political attitudes and relationships within Liverpool. It helped to encourage economic confidence and investment. It improved relationships between government and the city, since they had a combined interest in the dock being successful. It encouraged other investors to see the market potential of Liverpool city centre. The equally iconic Liverpool One complex would not have happened without the revitalised waterfront. The renaissance of Albert Dock encouraged confidence, hope and investment. Its progress was part of the explanation of the corresponding political progress of and within Liverpool in the years since. In 2018 its significance and role was symbolised by it being appointed Royal Albert Dock Liverpool.

'It was a turning point – the city turned away completely from a preoccupation with welfare to the economic regeneration of the city centre.' – Alan Chape, former assistant chief executive, Liverpool City Council

City Challenge was the second crucial piece in the jigsaw of Liverpool's normalisation and renaissance. This was the first attempt to fix a part of Liverpool beyond the waterfront. It not only led the way in regeneration at the time but was to become an even more important part of the city twenty years later as the foundation of Knowledge Quarter Liverpool. It was a very ambitious initiative in an area of significant neglect, trying to deliver a property-based regeneration programme in a recession. The national City Challenge programme had been invented by Michael Heseltine. It was different from urban regeneration initiatives that preceded it. It had wider goals. It adopted a more expansive definition of the urban problem. It recognised the importance of its different dimensions, economic, social and environmental. Setting the tone for much urban policy during this period, the money was allocated not primarily on need but on a competitive basis, and a variety of criteria including opportunity and likely delivery. The comprehensive approach and emphasis on decentralisation was a significant departure from earlier initiatives. Local authorities were given a lead role but had to work in partnership with other public, private and community groups. The teams had to have well-defined areas, tackle economic, physical and social issues, and have small teams and management committees drawn from all partners. The funds were relatively modest at £37.5 million for five years, but were intended to draw together public and private money. The initiative is commonly regarded as one of the best examples of urban policy in the UK's experience. It had a major impact upon Liverpool – the place, the people, the partnership, its processes – as the major evaluation by Hilary Russell, on which this account is based, clearly demonstrated.[7]

Liverpool was one of 11 cities that were given Challenge status in 1991. The bid had the support of 37 major partners, who stayed involved throughout. The area chosen was just on the eastern edge of the city centre, which had significant architecture and huge economic opportunities but was surrounded by areas of great need. It had huge potential but had never had any regeneration support in the past, and so might attract government interest. The area was highly visible publicly and politically. It contained a series of anchor institutions in retail, commerce, culture, health and education – including the universities, hospitals, theatre and orchestra. And it involved a range of partners attracted by the potential impact that could be achieved by attracting private-sector investment. But it had major physical and economic problems. The area had had a series of previous initiatives but they had not been very systematic or coordinated. It had few residents but over 900 buildings, many of which had lost their original economic functions.

What did it achieve?

Liverpool City Challenge faced some intractable economic, physical and social problems with modest financial and organisational resources against a history of failed initiatives but high expectations. But it worked and contributed enormously to Liverpool's first steps towards recovery. By 1997 the area had undergone a dramatic change in its physical appearance. Its prominent listed buildings, which had long been eyesores, had been refurbished and had end users. Challenge brought activity in many of the growth areas in education, the arts and cultural industries, hotel and leisure, residential, retail, health and professional services. It brought new businesses, residents and visitors to the area. It diversified the economic base without threatening activity elsewhere in the city centre. It encouraged city centre living and a new night-time economy. It encouraged greater market confidence, improved gateways into the city centre and a better living and working environment.

It delivered over 2,800 jobs, 300 business start-ups, 150,000 square metres of new and improved floor space, reclaimed 13 hectares of land and attracted over £112 million in private-sector investment. It encouraged the redevelopment of London Road and Queen Square and created new public transport routes through the area. It brought Blackburne House Women's Educational and Technology Centre into being and started the Liverpool Institute for Performing Arts. It refurbished the Philharmonic concert hall. It converted Lime Street Chambers into use as flats for university students. It delivered important environmental improvement in the Georgian Canning Street area. On the business front it created training and recruitment schemes, encouraged business associations and through its training programmes increased neighbourhood capacity and their engagement in regeneration partnerships.

The legacy of Challenge went beyond its individual products. It helped to change political attitudes and relationships in the city centre. The board was appointed by Peter Bounds and was made up of three public-sector members, three private-sector and three community interest representatives. Its chief executive, John Flamson, argued that to have such a representative board was hugely significant in Liverpool at that time. Politicians were excluded from the board. In fact this was virtually a condition on which the city received the funding, because of the continued distrust of the city council by the Conservative government. However, two years into City Challenge, Flamson asked the government to allow council members on the board. It agreed, saying that the city council had been 'rehabilitated'.

John Flamson was a key player in Challenge, but he served in virtually every part of the Liverpool city-making scene at various points in his career. He worked in the county council, the city council, the MDC, City Challenge, the Government Office for Merseyside and European Objective 1 and finally the University of Liverpool. In all those jobs, but especially as chief executive of Challenge, Flamson exuded confidence, ambition and foresight, refusing to be pigeonholed and constantly raising the sights of the city's decision makers. He broke the mould of the bureaucrat and was a classic example of the public entrepreneur who seemed to be in at the start of even the most unpropitious initiatives that were to flourish later. Under Bounds's and Flamson's leadership, Challenge also helped change the way in which Liverpool worked, creating new structures and processes for delivering regeneration and linking physical and economic renewal with local people. It encouraged partnership working in a city that had traditionally found this hard to do and that had been municipalist by instinct through the 1980s. It encouraged both community and private-sector engagement in the city – which again had been absent in earlier decades. Its partnership model of working in Liverpool was adopted both by Europe and the national government in later regeneration initiatives. It played honest broker in a city where relationships had been badly fractured. And it was more entrepreneurial and business-focused than earlier delivery vehicles.

Much done – but much more to do

City Challenge started the recovery process in Liverpool city centre, but when it ended in 1997 it was in no sense complete. Market confidence had increased and brought investment. But there had not yet been significant increases in land values or commercial rent levels. The programme had a huge impact on the physical condition of the area, but its wider impact on the lives and careers of people in and near the area was uncertain. It had found ways of reconnecting marginalised groups with the labour market, but its impact on deep-rooted unemployment was modest. City Challenge was a good news story for Liverpool, but it underlined some important challenges and limitations for the longer-term future. It raised confidence and investment, but whether that would continue after the initiative, especially given the demise of the MDC at the same time, remained uncertain. It had underlined the importance of the city centre to Liverpool's wider economy, but it raised the question of whether its importance was sufficiently recognised and would be sustained. This was crucial: 92,000 people worked in the city centre in offices, shops, hotels, restaurants, higher education, tourism and leisure. It was the focus of the city's cultural life and a key to its external image and identity. Challenge was a success but it only covered a part of the city centre. It would need a strong delivery vehicle to ensure that progress was continued across a wider area after Challenge was gone.

Challenge was a crucial element in normalising Liverpool's politics and its political culture. It had shown that it was possible to have real transformation of an area. It showed how a relatively small organisation could act as a catalyst and have a greater impact than by working on its own. It delivered many important projects and shaped many important relationships. By the early 1990s, partnership had become a key mechanism for regeneration in the city. This development was crowned by the formation in 1995 of the Liverpool Partnership Group, which brought together the chief executives of 18 public, private and voluntary bodies including, for example, the city council, the Government Office for Merseyside, the police, English Partnerships, the housing corporation, the Liverpool Housing Action Trust, the employment service, the Benefits Agency and the local universities. The key question for Liverpool was whether it could build upon and sustain that progress.

Remaking Liverpool, Act 3: enter Europe

'1994 and Objective 1 was massive – not a bit but a lot. It was a Godsend.'
– Alan Chape

The most significant impact on Liverpool and its economic renaissance at this time was made by the European Commission, which gave Merseyside Objective 1 status in 1994. This changed everything. Merseyside had had EU structural funds since the 1980s, and between 1989 and 1993 it was an Objective 2 region. But during the 1990s its GDP dropped below 75% of the national average, making it eligible for Objective 1 status, which brought much higher sums of money. Between 1994 and 2006 Merseyside received £1.5 billion from the Commission. Gaining this status was not straightforward. It had to be agreed not only by the European Commission but also by the British government. The European Commission was supportive but believed that a Conservative government would be reluctant to acknowledge that any part of the UK was poor enough to need support from Europe. The city had to press its case. Lobbying by the council leader Harry Rimmer, without very much support from sceptical local authority leaders across Merseyside, got the status awarded. Rimmer argued that the UK's entry into Europe and the loss of Commonwealth trade had badly damaged Liverpool's economy and that Europe owed the city financial aid to help it deal with the consequences. The status was awarded in July 1993, with Michael Heseltine helping to persuade the Cabinet to approve Merseyside's designation. This had a major impact on the resources that came into the city, but also the way in which decisions about the economic future of Liverpool were made. The European Commission was a huge contributor to Liverpool's renaissance and its senior representative, Graeme Meadows, was a key figure. He was another breath of fresh air and a non-bureaucratic public servant who constantly challenged the city to behave differently and creatively – but also supported its cause with his political masters in Brussels.

The plan – called the Single Programming Document – was agreed in July 1994. It had seven strategic objectives: developing existing manufacturing industry by encouraging investment in key corporate sectors; investing in people to increase job opportunities, stimulate enterprise and upgrade skills; enhancing technology and improving links between research and development organisations and industry; increasing job opportunities for people in the most deprived communities through 'pathways to integration'; helping Merseyside become a major gateway between Europe and the rest of the world; developing the city region's strengths in culture, media and tourism and attracting more visitors to the region; and encouraging sustainable development.

This was a wider, more strategic approach than had been undertaken in the past to the future economy of Liverpool and the city region. In a way it reinstated the city-region wide approach that had been lost when the Thatcher government abolished the Merseyside County Council in 1986, with the accompanying loss of capacity, intelligence, vision and ambition for the wider Liverpool economy. It involved European, national and local government; it involved a large number of public, private and community partners; and it had significant capacity to deliver, based in the Government Office for Merseyside. The first programme was too wide with too many initiatives. But in the second phase it concentrated on a smaller set of strategic objectives with a more streamlined delivery system. And again it worked.

Liverpool's continuing recovery at this time was rooted in several factors – rising public expenditure, better local political leadership, and a revived investment market for cities. But European programmes and money played a big part. However, Europe brought much more than money. The Commission invested heavily in key infrastructure projects and helped to modernise the economy. It encouraged a model of community involvement in decision making that became a prototype for Europe. It encouraged partners to work at a city-region level long before UK politicians discovered the idea. Most importantly, it asked what Liverpool's purpose would be in future. That simple economic challenge hugely changed the city's mind-set, forcing it to be more expansive and more ambitious – if also more realistic.[8]

Waterfront, 2004
Image courtesy of the University of Liverpool

What did it deliver?

The EU invested right across the city region, though it was concentrated in Liverpool at the heart of its economy. The programme had two phases and ran until 2006. It was the most significant public intervention, much greater than any comparable initiative by the UK government. The first round of Objective 1 invested £640 million. The second round spent £929 million. EU funds supported a huge number of investments and projects that were critical to the future of the Liverpool economy. It created almost 40,000 new jobs. It provided one third of a million training places for adults and over 60,000 for young people. Importantly the Commission promoted measures targeted at people at risk of permanent exclusion from the labour market. People living in areas with significant economic and social problems received a raft of measures providing 'pathways' to education, skills, training, jobs and involvement in designing, implementing and monitoring the initiatives funded in their areas. The money was delivered with the involvement of people living in 38 Area Partnerships, including representatives of public, private and, notably, community sectors.[9]

One of the largest investments of EU funds nationally was the Arena and Convention Centre, which received £60 million towards a total cost of £160 million and which subsequently flourished as a hugely successful part of the visitor and waterfront economy. The EU helped refurbish or restore 26 listed buildings. It invested £25 million in Liverpool John Lennon Airport and £15 million in a depressed area of the city centre, Ropewalks, which became a

Liverpool waterfront from the air, 2017
© Paul White – North West England/Alamy Stock Photo

Arena and
Convention
Centre
© McCoy Wynne
(mccoywynne.co.uk)

vibrant mixed-use area, and which subsequently encouraged the over £1.4 billion investment by Grosvenor Estates in the Liverpool One project next door. It heavily supported the knowledge economy, including the Bio-Manufacturing Centre, Liverpool Innovation Park and the Centre for Materials Discovery. It invested £9 million in the Liverpool School of Tropical Medicine, which helped it to attract £35 million in research funding from the Gates Foundation, and £11 million in Liverpool Science Park, which now has over 70 firms in life science and IT industries. It created the £70 million Merseyside Special Investment Fund, which leveraged £274 million of private-sector investment. It supported Liverpool Neighbourhood Regeneration Programme, a £35 million project which combined ERDF and ESF to support a wide range of activities across 11 deprived communities in the city. More than 5,200 residents moved from unemployment into work.

The programme was expensive, visible and ambitious. It was subject to a number of evaluations to see what it had achieved, whether it had added value and what were the secrets of its success. A key review was the Liverpool Mayor's Commission in 2013.[10] It was very positive. It argued that EU funding, because of its longevity, certainty and ability to encourage the private sector to invest, had succeeded where national government funding had not. The seven-year EU funding cycle allowed long-term planning. Unlike EU funding, the bulk of national funding went into social costs, such as housing, education and welfare. Little was left for capital investment. EU funding was less risk-averse than national government and a series of high-risk critical projects had been successfully funded. The review accepted that Liverpool still lagged behind the rest of the UK in terms of productivity, unemployment and rates of employment. But on all of these key economic indicators Liverpool had outperformed the UK over the previous fifteen years to close the economic gap. GVA per head had grown from 90% to 98% of the UK average. 50,000 jobs were created in the city region. Unemployment had fallen from double the UK average to 1.6 times the UK rate. The employment rate had risen from 56% to 60% while the national employment rate had slipped from 73% to 71%.

The report argued that Objective 1 had helped to grow economic sectors that were important to the Liverpool economy and had given it a competitive economic advantage. It had encouraged partnership working. It had engaged higher education and raised the profile of the knowledge economy. It demonstrated the potential of the visitor economy to sustain jobs and growth. It concentrated investment in areas where Liverpool had genuine competitive advantage. It provided revenue support alongside capital investment to increase sustainability. It had supported SMEs. It had provided venture capital funds for high-risk ventures. It had supported hard-to-reach groups. It had helped to: increase land values and rental levels; create a busier and more attractive city centre and retail offer; transform Liverpool's internationally recognised waterfront; increase the quality and quantity of Liverpool's hotels; and increase visitor numbers and improve perceptions of the city.

It wasn't perfect

There were some limitations to the programme. Initially there was too much concern with managing the process rather than delivering projects. There was a tendency to give all partners a share of the cake rather than following strategic priorities. The programme was unwieldy. But many of the problems in the first round of Objective 1 were tackled in the second round. It was rationalised and streamlined, more strategic, more tightly managed and monitored. It had fewer economic drivers and fewer priorities. There was greater focus upon the city centre. There was greater focus on encouraging business growth. There was more attention on educational under-attainment and linking the employment needs of deprived communities to areas with the greatest potential.

'We could not continue to spread the money so thinly in Round 2. We decided to invest in strategic capital projects that would have long lasting effects. We tried to push the economy toward a different future – high tech, tourism, knowledge, professional and financial services and to attract people to Liverpool including politicians to challenge their old perceptions. And it worked.' – Professor Michael Brown, former vice chancellor LJMU, chair Objective 1 Strategy Committee

The most thoughtful assessment of Europe's strategic contribution to Liverpool city region was made by Richard Evans.[11] He argued that the programme had contributed to both policies and performance in Merseyside. It encouraged partners to look critically at the assets, opportunities and challenges of the whole city region. It encouraged working across local authority boundaries. Its willingness to involve local communities ensured more local solutions to problems. It encouraged greater collaboration between the city, universities and local businesses and a greater focus on graduate employment and retention. It helped to increase inward investment partly by providing priority sites. It encouraged and funded the marketing agency of the city region. Although initially the programme was too dominated by the public sector, the private sector did get more involved over time through the Merseyside Special Investment Fund, its venture capital fund for SMEs. It encouraged local firms to engage more with local community groups on employment. It encouraged the engagement of local communities and tried to provide economic opportunities in deprived areas in a pioneering attempt to give socially excluded people a stake in the city region's future.[12] It forced regeneration agencies, especially in Liverpool, to adapt their mainstream programmes to local priorities. The scale of social exclusion remained large given the city's long-term structural challenges, but there were significant successes in physical terms.

The balance sheet on Europe

'Europe and Graeme Meadows believed in and trusted Liverpool more than government. He took a gamble when government would just faff around.' – Ged Fitzgerald, former chief executive, Liverpool City Council

European funding was neither the first nor the only lifeline thrown to Liverpool. But the sheer scale of Objective 1 funding caused a step-change in its confidence and gave its leaders the stability of funding over a long period to plan for change. Huge progress was made in a relatively short space of time. The place moved from a vulnerable post-imperial to a stronger and more diverse economy embracing knowledge, science and innovation, culture and tourism. Its physical transformation of landmark public spaces, strategic investment areas and key transport hubs had positioned it as a place where people wanted to live, work and play. European investment in the physical and cultural assets of the area raised its image and profile with both visitors and potential investors. It internationalised the city once again. It made Liverpool in its own and others' eyes a modern European city and laid the foundations for the full development of that status in the next decade. It underlined what is at risk with the prospect of Brexit. Liverpool paid a heavy price when the UK joined the European Community in 1973, as it diminished many of its Commonwealth trading links. But twenty years later Europe made a huge contribution to the continuing renaissance of Liverpool city region. It helped change attitudes and political relationships. It raised Liverpool's aspirations. It raised the tone of the debate. It raised strategic questions about Liverpool's future. And it put its money where its mouth was. Europe mattered and it made a difference.[13]

'It was the best thing we ever did. No other regeneration scheme was as ambitious or as successful.' – Peter Bounds, former chief executive, Liverpool City Council

Most of the initiatives discussed so far were focused on Liverpool city centre, although Europe also operated across the whole city region. The Speke Garston Programme, set up in the mid-1990s, was in a different kind of place – the engine room of the traditional manufacturing area in the city, with huge challenges but significant opportunities. I argued in 2000 that it was one of the most interesting and important initiatives in the city.[14] The combination of a Single Regeneration Budget Partnership and the Speke Garston Development Company funded jointly by the city council and English Partnerships was beginning to have a major impact on a once derelict industrial area. An industrial and business park was taking shape. The environment was being transformed. 7,000 houses had been shifted from the local authority to a housing company. Ford Jaguar had invested heavily in its old factory and had turned a basket-case into an icon. Its investment had been matched by biotechnology and pharmaceutical investment by Medeva, Ely Lilly and Glaxo-Wellcome. Capital Bank had invested substantially and the original 1930s art deco airport terminal had been transformed into a hotel and leisure centre, with a new airport being built two miles away. Engagement by the Partnership and Development Company with the local community and employers meant that many of the jobs were going to local

Eastern Avenue bus terminus from Speke Boulevard (Ford's Road), February 1972. The sign reads 'Any person found damaging this fence will be prosecuted'
© Tom Speke (municipaldreams. wordpress.com)

The leafy
Victorian Sefton
Park in south
Liverpool, 2
miles away from
Speke
© Ant Clausen
(antclausen.com)

people. The subsequent independent review of the Speke Garston initiative by Hilary Russell, on which the following account is based, confirmed my initial judgement.[15]

What challenges did Speke Garston face?

The Speke Garston area covered over 1,000 hectares seven miles to the south of Liverpool city centre, running along the Mersey. It was an area of strategic importance to the city and formed its southern gateway. It had the largest concentration of manufacturing industry in the city and was already an important base for large and small businesses. The presence of automotive and pharmaceutical industries strengthened Speke Garston's case for investment. However, it had the classic social, economic and environmental problems that sprang from decades of deterioration: industrial and commercial decline; contaminated land, extensive dereliction and outdated industrial property; degraded housing, environment and townscape; high levels of unemployment, low income, low skills and educational attainment, poor health and crime; and a poor image among both potential investors and residents. Speke was one of the largest self-contained housing estates in the country, with 5,800 dwellings. Unemployment in 1996 was

21.5%, above the city region level of 18.5% and the national average of 9.5%; 48% of the unemployed were long-term unemployed. It suffered from poor housing maintenance and repair, few local facilities and poor public transport links. Less than one in six families owned a car, with half the households officially living in poverty. Poor levels of educational achievement had created a cycle of deprivation. It desperately needed help and attention.

How was it set up?

The initiative stemmed from Liverpool's failure to obtain from the government a second City Challenge for the Speke Garston area in 1993. Harry Rimmer's view was that the government felt that Liverpool had already had enough public money. But he thought the project so important and the City Challenge bid so powerful that the city council should try to do it without direct government support. He persuaded the regional director of the newly formed English Partnerships, Jim Gill, who was later chief executive of Liverpool Vision in the city centre and another key player in the regeneration of Liverpool, to join with the city council in a Speke Garston Development Company (SGDC). Rimmer had already been in discussions with the chief executive at Ford about a plan to regenerate the area and knew there was private-sector support for the proposal. English Partnerships had identified Speke Garston as one of its national priorities when it was first set up in 1994. The company was a joint venture between Liverpool City Council and English Partnerships, the first that English Partnerships made with a local authority, and it operated between 1996 and 2003. English Partnerships held 80% of the company shares and the city council 20%. It had a small senior management team that reported to a board drawn from English Partnerships and Liverpool City Council, with an independent chair, Ray O'Brien, a powerful figure who had been chief executive of Merseyside County Council before it was abolished. Its chief executive, Bob Lane, was an experienced and respected player in the regeneration of Liverpool who had been assistant chief executive of the MDC. It was a quality combination, typically a crucial ingredient of success in regeneration vehicles.

The company worked in close partnership with a Single Regeneration Budget project that had been established in Speke in 1995, the Speke Garston Partnership (SGP), when it won £17 million funding from government for a five-year programme. This was extended for a further five years with another £4 million in 1999. The Partnership was designed to operate alongside the SGDC to act as an 'envelope' for the company's physical regeneration programme. The arrangement allowed a two-pronged approach, with the SGDC undertaking the physical regeneration and the SGP the social – focusing on education, training, childcare, community safety, health and the needs of the community and voluntary sector. In particular it was designed to help local people to access training and job opportunities from the inward investment brought by the SGDC. The SGDC, set up in July 1996, began its first formal year of operation in April 1997. This timing of the initiative was right. City Challenge in the city centre was coming to an end. The Speke Garston project was able to reap the benefits of its partnership working and to attract employees who had gained experience there. Also, it was important that Liverpool maintained the momentum created by City Challenge and increased the perception that the city was getting its act together strategically and could deliver big initiatives and projects. The model anticipated and to an extent influenced later government policy initiatives.

What did it achieve?

The SGDC had a major impact upon the economy of the area. It brought in £230 million of private-sector investment and £100 million of public-sector investment, including £15 million of EU Objective 1 funding. It improved over 190 hectares of land. It created 230,000 sq. metres of new or improved industrial and commercial floor space. It created or safeguarded 5,600 jobs. It established Boulevard Industry Park, a cluster of suppliers for Jaguar and biopharma-ceutical companies including Chiron Vaccines, Medimmune and Powderjet. It established Estuary Commerce Park, which housed Riverside Group's head office, Halifax, Bank of Scotland, Liverpool Blood Centre, DHL, Powder Systems, Classic Couverture, National Bio-manufacturing Centre as well as Venture Point Business Park. It started the Matchworks redevelopment, the conversion of the former Bryant and May match factory, together with a new building, Matchbox. The whole development created over 2,100 jobs. It oversaw the conversion of the former listed art deco airport terminal building into a hotel and Hangar 1 into a leisure centre and new restaurant on the old airport site. It undertook environ-mental improvements to Speke Boulevard and Speke Road, providing footpaths,

The Matchworks
Business
Park, Garston,
Liverpool
Image courtesy of
Stephen Mason via
Wikimedia Commons

cycle ways, and 250,000 new trees, shrubs and plants. It refurbished the old Liverpool airport aerodrome for offices and light industry. The Development Company won the BURA regeneration award in 2001, the RICS Outstanding Achievement in Regeneration Award in 2002 and the Royal Bank of Scotland Regeneration Award in 2006.

The Partnership had particularly good results in terms of employment, people gaining qualifications, new business start-ups, support of voluntary organisations and people engaged in voluntary work, and childcare. It received £126 million of public-sector funding in total. SGP's total leverage was £309 million. The Partnership delivered substantial physical change by winning Estates Renewal Challenge Funding, which enabled the establishment of South Liverpool Housing and brought £130 million into the area for housing renewal and planned maintenance. It provided new community facilities including Garston Community House, a new swimming pool and leisure centre, and Garston Urban Village Hall. 230 new private-sector homes and 35 social housing units were initially built in addition to a sheltered housing scheme. It created the new Mersey Retail Park. It provided Speke with a new comprehensive school in a campus with other services and amenities. It started a new district centre for Speke and a new bus station. It strengthened the community sector through the founding of new groups, by training and capacity building, with grants from the Community and Voluntary Sector Development Fund and by helping groups get major funding. Before SGP, despite the strength of the local private sector, there was little sense of a coherent business community. The creation of the Business Leaders' Group changed that. There was, however, less improvement in local residents' social and economic status. There were improvements, but not necessarily very different from the city-wide changes.

Why did it work?

'The way the people worked was brilliant. It was the template for the later city centre renaissance.' – Claire McColgan, director, Culture Liverpool

Speke Garston had a unique delivery mechanism. The Partnership supplied the 'software' of social regeneration to complement the 'hardware' of the Development Company's economic regeneration. The SGDC needed the Partnership to provide more attractive inward investment packages, including customised training and recruitment support. The SGDC helped the Partnership's efforts to raise educational attainment and skill levels and its wider work in environmental improvement. The Partnership's business support work gave a higher profile to SMEs, strengthening the area's economic base and making it more attractive to investors. The Partnership benefited from the SGDC's physical programme. Apart from bringing new jobs to the area, the infrastructure and development work was very visible. People could see that time, energy and resources were being invested. The evidence of change generated greater local confidence and served to raise individual and communal aspirations. The Partnership's programme balanced the social and the economic. They also worked closely with government as well as with public, private, voluntary and community sectors locally. Their successful track record led to confidence, people listening to them and trusting them with new projects.

Charlie Parker, who was chief executive of the Partnership and who subsequently moved to become Director of Regeneration in Liverpool City Council, argued that what happened in Speke Garston was the prototype for the rest of the city. For him the key ingredients were 'Clarity, vision and purpose. Strong leadership from the public and private sectors. The coalescence of national and local events. It moved from grant led to private sector investment. It gave the private sector real hope – you could feel and touch the confidence.' The chief executive of SGDC, Bob Lane, described it as 'the best regeneration machine I've ever worked in'. Its success, in his view, was down to a very experienced, top-quality team being in the right place at the right time, with Liverpool starting to recover, the national economy recovering from a major recession at the beginning of the 1990s and the fact that the Company did good work.

The Speke Garston project was another important part of the Liverpool jigsaw, remaking some of its worn-out infrastructure and relationships to turn around a critical part of Liverpool's industrial and manufacturing economy. The current success and investment of Jaguar Land Rover – a global leading company – would surely never have occurred without the foundations laid by this initiative. In both the way it did its business and its impact on the ground, this was one of the most important phases of Liverpool's renaissance. It got one more bit of Liverpool closer to being a normal place. Again major public-sector funding had attracted substantial private-sector investment – and it delivered.

'City Challenge was a partnership between local players. Speke Garston was the first real partnership in the UK between national and local government. That is why it was so successful and so important.' – Jim Gill, former regional director, English Partnerships

BOOM – changing the signals from the private sector about Liverpool

The projects I have discussed so far were essentially public-sector initiated, led or funded. That was in keeping with the mood and feel of the times in the city. Nevertheless, this period of normalisation was marked by a shift in the role and attitudes of the private sector in the city. During the 1980s the private sector had been deterred from getting involved in city politics because of the divisive and poisonous political atmosphere in the city. But many of them, like other people, were shocked if not frightened by how near Liverpool had come to going over the edge of the abyss. During the late 1980s a series of initiatives emerged to try to get the private sector into a debate about the city – partly to protect their own economic interests and partly to promote the longer-term interests of the city itself. The Bishop and the Archbishop of Liverpool, David Sheppard and Derek Worlock, who at the most difficult moments in the 1980s were the only representatives of the city that the government would believe or put any trust in, had set up their Michaelmas group of private-sector players, which met to discuss the problems facing the city.[16] The higher education leaders – Graeme Davies, the vice chancellor of the University of Liverpool, and Peter Toyne, the rector of Liverpool Polytechnic – were also key players who provided important personal and institutional commitment and investment to the city at a difficult time. However, the most significant and influential of the groups was a private-sector-led group, Business Opportunities on Merseyside (BOOM). It was as important for the tone it set and the mood it tried to encourage as for any immediate and direct impact upon the economics or politics of the place. It was symptomatic of the cultural changes that were taking place in the city in the post-Militant period. It was set up in 1987 and changed into the Mersey Partnership in 1993. This private-sector marketing organisation lasted until 2015 when it became part of the Liverpool city region Local Enterprise Partnership. So BOOM started a long thread of private-sector marketing and promotional activities in Liverpool.[17]

Its moving spirit was Geoffrey Piper, an accountant with KPMG who had moved to the city in the 1980s. He was almost a lone southern voice speaking up for the Scousers then. He started his private-sector initiative at a time when being positive about Liverpool seemed an oxymoron. But in his dogged and charming manner he got many people onside and helped to start the long way back for Liverpool. His organisation was not a deliverer of real products, but its constant programme to talk up the city did help change the mood music about Liverpool. He became the orchestrator and cheerleader for the private sector in the city. He argued that pessimism had not only affected the marginalised and disadvantaged communities, but also plagued the city's politicians and its business community. He wanted to try to attract private-sector investment into the city, by building on the regeneration that had taken place in Albert Dock, Wavertree Technology Park and Stockbridge Village. He formed a small committee of private-sector people, many of whom, like him, were relatively recent arrivals in the city with perhaps less baggage than long-time residents. Piper lobbied these individuals and institutions and got BOOM launched in 1987.

BOOM had 140 paying members from companies of all shapes and sizes as well as the endorsement and support of a range of public-sector organisations, including the Merseyside Task Force, the MDC and the university. Its financial and human resources were modest, but it got a lot of goodwill and in-kind support from the private sector. As Piper observed, it was crucial that there had been a change of leadership in the local authority, which was trying to rebuild relationships with government but also the private sector. BOOM's aim was to promote the professional and cultural assets of the region and to attract long-term capital investment. It tried to persuade investors and decision makers to come to Liverpool to see personally that its public image was not accurate and to change their view of the city as an investment opportunity. It began a lobbying and promotional process for the city, presenting its cultural and lifestyle assets nationally and internationally. It lobbied ministers and government. It cultivated MPs. It lobbied senior civil servants. It arranged fact-finding visits by private-sector investors to the city. It produced a series of glossy promotional documents. It got positive articles about the city into the national press. It got prime ministerial, ministerial and royal endorsements for its various annual reports.

An external review of BOOM in 1991 argued that it had helped change internal and external perceptions of the city. It had created trust and consensus and joint working between the previously divided private and public sectors. It had boosted the morale of Merseyside. It had been a focal point for the local and national media. It had produced high-quality promotional material for investors which probably contributed to some investment. However, it was becoming clear even to its own leaders that BOOM was in danger of becoming a victim of its own success – asked to do too many things without the resources required for the scale of the job. It was obvious that a small, private-sector-led initiative could not produce the scale of the effort that would be needed to capitalise upon the political and to some extent economic recovery that was beginning to take place in Liverpool. There had to be a more powerful, well-resourced body that had stronger working links with the public sector.

In 1993 it was agreed to create a new organisation, the Mersey Partnership, which would absorb the marketing activities of the local authorities, BOOM and the Merseyside Tourism Authority. BOOM's pilot work was done. Its staff transferred to the Partnership and Geoffrey Piper remained its deputy chair. The Mersey Partnership lasted until the creation by government of Local Enterprise Partnerships in 2010. It would be wrong to exaggerate the impact of BOOM, but the mere fact of its existence was an indicator of the changing mood in Liverpool at this crucial time. It was small in scale and informal in nature and could not claim to have delivered major investment projects. But it contributed to the changes of political culture within the city and helped improve perceptions of Liverpool on the part of investors and national politicians. It demonstrated that the private sector should and could re-engage in Liverpool city politics and economics. It was a small but important start on the journey that the city took back to normalcy. Bigger things would follow, but a precedent had been set.

So where was Liverpool at the end of the decade of normalisation?

The four big city projects discussed in this chapter had helped place Liverpool in a very different position at the end of the decade from where it had been at the beginning. In different ways in different areas of the city, they had delivered success on the ground. They had delivered quality. They had encouraged partnership working. They had involved the private sector. They had built good working relationships between the local authority, government and the European Commission. They had improved the city's image internally and externally. Investment in the waterfront, the city centre and Speke Garston on the edge of the city all played to the city's economic performance and potential. At the end of the decade, parts of Liverpool looked and were very different. It had something to go on. It was more stable politically. It was working more in partnership. It was no longer a ho-hoper. The city had been normalised in many ways. The remaking of the post-imperial city was underway.[18]

But the job had only been started. The city's agenda was still shaped by national and European governments. The local authority had not improved its processes or performance as much as was needed. The remade areas were only parts – if important ones – of the city. The ruling Labour group had run out of ambition and energy. It lacked a clear vision of where Liverpool overall was going. Nobody had outlined a bigger picture for the future of the city except the European Commission. The fundamental economic and social challenges remained across much of the city. There was much more to do in 1997, as a New Labour Party took control of national government with a very different agenda for Britain's cities. But this presented a further opportunity for a normalised Liverpool to remake itself and aspire to become a premier European city.[19]

Notes

1   Michael Parkinson, 'Liverpool – de la crise à la régénération urbain', *Les Cahiers de la Recherche Architecturale*, 30/31 (1992).

2   Cocks, op cit., p. 189.

3   Cocks, op. cit., p. 189.

4   Michael Parkinson, 'Proud City Down in the Dumps', *The Times*, 25 June 1991.

5   Peter Bounds, 'Is This a Way to Run a City?', *Municipal Journal*, 22 (1994).

6   Michael Parkinson and Alex Lord, *Albert Dock: What Part in Liverpool's Continuing Renaissance?* (Heseltine Institute, University of Liverpool, 2017); Richard Meegan, 'Urban Development Corporations, Urban Entrepreneurialism and Locality: The Merseyside Development Corporation', in Rob Imrie and Huw Thomas (eds), *British Urban Policy* (Sage, 1999); Michael Parkinson, 'Urban Development Corporations', in Michael Campbell (ed.), *Local Economic Policy* (Cassell, 1990); Michael Parkinson and John Dawson, 'Physical Renewal, Accountability and Economic Challenge', in Michael Keith and Alasdair Rogers (eds), *Hollow Promises? Policy, Theory and Practice in the Inner City* (Mansell, 1990); Michael Parkinson, 'Les agences de développement urbain Britannique', *Les Annales Recherche Urbain*, 48 (1990).

7   Hilary Russell, *Liverpool City Challenge: Final Evaluation Report* (European Institute for Urban Affairs, 1997); Hilary Russell, Michael Parkinson et al., *City Challenge: Interim National Evaluation* (HMSO, 1996); Michael Parkinson, 'City Challenge – A New Strategy for Britain's Cities?', *Policy Studies*, 3 (1993); Simoni Davoudi and Patsy Healey, 'City Challenge: Sustainable Policy or Temporary Gesture?', *Environment and Planning C: Government and Policy*, 13 (1995); Lucy de Groot, 'City Challenge: Competing in the Urban Regeneration Game', *Local Economy*, 7.3 (1992).

8   Michael Parkinson, 'Stand Up and Be Counted for Europe', *Town and Country Planning* (June/July 2015).

9   Karen Hibbert, Peris Jones and Richard Meegan, 'Tackling Social Exclusion; The Role of Social Capital in Urban Regeneration on Merseyside – From Mistrust to Trust?', *European Planning Studies*, 9.2 (2001).

10 Liverpool City Council, *The Mayor's Commission on Europe* (2013).

11 Richard Evans, 'The Merseyside Objective 1 Programme: Exemplar of Coherent City Regional Planning or Cautionary Tale?', *European Planning Studies*, 10.4 (2002).

12 Richard Meegan and Alison Mitchell, '"It's not community round here, its neighbourhood": Neighbourhood Change and Cohesion in Urban Regeneration Policies', *Urban Studies*, 38.12 (2001).

13 Government Office for the North West, *EU and Merseyside – the Objective 1 Programme* (2008).

14 Parkinson, *Parliamentary Brief*, op. cit.

15 Hilary Russell et al., *The Speke Garston Partnership: End of Scheme Evaluation* (European Institute for Urban Affairs, 2004).

16 Sheppard and Worlock, op. cit.

17 Geoffrey Piper, *Doom and Gloom and then a BOOM* (Heseltine Institute, University of Liverpool, 2018).

18 Michael Parkinson, 'Liverpool, déclin et renaissance', in Jacques Beauchard (ed.), *Espaces-Projets Atlantiques: Convertir les périphéries en façades* (1995).

19 Michael Parkinson, 'The Quality of Mersey', *The Observer*, 4 February 1997.

CHAPTER FOUR

The rise of the aspiring premier European city, 1998–2010

By the late 1990s Liverpool was closer to its leadership's aspiration to be a normal city. At this time a number of factors combined to improve its prospects of further progress. First, a New Labour government was elected in 1997 with a commitment and the capacity generated by an economic boom to increase public expenditure, tackle social deprivation in UK cities and address regional inequalities. Secondly, Liverpool's politics changed. The Labour group that had run the city for fifteen years was dramatically thrown out of office in 1998, just a year after a Labour government had been elected. The Labour group and leadership had run out of ideas and energy. The new Liberal Democrat administration took office with a very different, ambitious plan for Liverpool, to make it a premier European city, with the city centre as a key economic driver. Thirdly, there was a significant attempt to reorganise and make the local authority a modern efficient administration. Fourthly, the focus on the city centre was strengthened by the creation in 2001 of a city centre regeneration agency, Liverpool Vision. Finally, in 2003 Liverpool won and successfully delivered in 2008 the European Capital of Culture. These factors all underpinned Liverpool's renaissance.

During this 'golden age' for the city a Liberal Democrat administration successfully exploited the New Labour government's commitment to cities, the revived private-sector interest in city centre investment and large amounts of national and especially European funding to make dramatic physical, economic and cultural changes that dragged Liverpool into the mainstream of national and European cities. At that time in 2001 I wrote that even for a place that had turned many corners, there was evidence that Liverpool was putting its bad old

Central panel
of the Liverpool
Tapestry
© Sabena Jane
Blackbird/Alamy
Stock Photo

ways behind it as it attempted to become a leading European city.[1] In a Celtic city that could legendarily provoke an argument in an empty room, there were signs that peace had broken out. The politics were much improved. The public sector was talking to the private sector. Even the government no longer treated the city as a pariah.

Changing local authority performance and purpose

The first step in the process was that the city council began to get its act together. The continuity provided by a substantial majority for the Liberal Democrats and a leader with a clear vision of where he wanted to take the city helped. Crucial figures at the beginning of Liverpool's real renaissance were Mike Storey and David Henshaw, the leader and chief executive of the city, respectively, from 1998 to 2005 and 2006, when their paths diverged. Storey was a local politician and school headteacher who grew to become a statesman leading his city. Even though he confessed that he rather made up the idea of Liverpool as a premier European city on his way from an election broadcast at BBC Radio Merseyside to the Town Hall to claim his unexpected victory in 1998, he did see what was involved and what was necessary to give Liverpool back ambition. But Storey was realistic as well as ambitious. 'It was a gradual process not a metamorphosis. It was a question of polishing the jewels we had got – the city centre, the university. Visions are the assassins of idealism. You have to be rooted in reality and authentic.' Henshaw was a dynamic if occasionally divisive figure who knew what was wanted and how to get it. Between them they played a crucial role in turning round the city council's services, winning Capital of Culture and persuading the Duke of Westminster to invest in the huge Liverpool One city centre retail project. They gave leadership, ambition and confidence to the city at a time when it was possible to make a difference to its trajectory. This was matched by the drastic restructuring of the city council, with new senior officers who recognised that the council had not been good at delivery and had to do much better in future. One of the city's traditional problems – that good staff would not go and work for it – was changing, encouraged by large salary increases. There were some early signs of progress.

As David Robertson wrote at the time, behind its turbulent political façade, Liverpool had struggled for years to establish a post-industrial sense of purpose, lacking leaders prepared to undertake the strategic self-review essential for its renaissance.[2] In his judgement that was changing. Stable political control was allowing the ruling Liberal Democrat Party to carry out its mandate by encouraging a management culture committed to municipal modernisation. Uninhibited by reliance on labour unions, they had shifted local authority emphasis from the protection of municipal jobs to the management of better-quality services and to regeneration. Politically the city council was more reliably led. Its affairs were more efficiently administered and service standards were slowly rising. Modest confidence was returning as investors and new residents relocated to city centre enterprises and waterfront apartments. The city was being trusted again. In Robertson's words, 'Liverpool is starting to think ahead rather than looking back all the time.'

How was this achieved? A key part was played by David Henshaw who was determined to improve the city council's performance internally and change its role externally, making it a partnership-oriented rather than a controlling public-sector organisation. When he took over the city council it had the highest council tax in the UK and its services were ranked the third worst. He argued that nobody would take the city council seriously as a key partner in the regeneration of the city if its own organisation was hopelessly inefficient. In his view there was

no overarching vision for what we were trying to do. There was no sense of what business we were in. It was a moribund organisation in many ways. It was the third from bottom performance of a local authority and it cost the most. Performance was atrocious, it was massively over-peopled. We were ankle deep in strategy documents, but we didn't do anything about them. So we had to mobilise things politically.[3]

He argued that the system could not be brought back under control by normal methods, only by shock and awe treatment. The previous chief executive, Peter Bounds, never had the political support to do what Henshaw did with Storey. They led a radical restructuring of the council, cutting the number of departments from eleven to five and instituting a voluntary severance scheme that led to a reduction from 23,000 to 19,000 employees in five years. They recruited a team of ambitious senior officers. They reorganised IT services and employment practices. They held the council tax stable for five years so that in 2004 it was the 57th not 3rd highest. The council won prizes for its 'one-stop shop' development. It made significant improvements in GCSE scores after the schools had almost been put in special measures in 1999. It improved the speed and quality of its special needs statementing, refuse collection, child protection case reviews, planning applications and business rates collection. The conduct of business had been sharpened. The council's executive had been slimmed down. Committee work had been streamlined. A Cabinet system had been established. Decision making had been speeded up. Crucially, the local authority had begun to carve out a useful role. It was actively leading city region economic regeneration and the promotion of a positive civic image. Their ambition to turn Liverpool into Britain's most business-friendly city had been a fanciful goal a few years back, but was now at least thinkable. The Audit Commission in 2002 endorsed this view, praising the city council for 'its powerful, compelling and ambitious vision for improvement and significant improvements in the level and quality of its services'. An external review of the local authority agreed, arguing that taking an organisation that was the subject of vilification and transforming it to the point where aspects of its service were held to be beacon sites of innovation and good practice was 'a success story measured against almost every management metrics and given the scale of reshaping involved … an impressively fast change process'.[4]

However, the review raised two longer-term concerns. Could the local authority sustain the momentum without innovating too much or exhausting its organisational capacity to deliver complex change? And could the dynamic chief executive adjust his management style to allow greater local leadership across the organisation? Both of these concerns were to prove prescient. The chief executive and the leader of the council fell out, in part because of Henshaw's very visible role, and their very successful partnership ended publicly and divisively in bitter tears. They left the authority in 2005 and 2006 respectively. It was a disappointment and a loss for the city. The leader and chief executive who followed them, Warren Bradley and Colin Hilton, found it challenging to maintain the momentum that the city had achieved. Just as the ruling Labour Party had a decade earlier, the Liberal Democrats ran out of energy by the end of the decade on its transformative agenda. But not before it had substantially improved the city council's performance and prospects.

'Liverpool was the hole in the middle of the Mersey polo. It was marooned and isolated. It was disconnected from the private sector.' – Sir David Henshaw

The real agenda for Storey and Henshaw was not the improvement of the city council. That was a necessary but not a sufficient condition for the transformation of the city. They wanted to raise Liverpool's performance, delivery, profile, reputation and ambition and make it a premier European city.[5] Although the terminology was new, it did reflect what Storey had identified as the city's problems and potential in the previous decade. It had been unambitious, introverted and not attuned to the needs and opportunities of the national and international market place. Two important projects symbolised their ambition and achievements. The first was the creation of a new city centre delivery vehicle, Liverpool Vision, which during the 2000s transformed Liverpool's city centre. The second was winning and delivering a hugely successful European Capital of Culture bid, which raised the profile, capacity and self-confidence of the city and dramatically improved its image as a city able to deliver quality prestige projects. Both changed the physical face of Liverpool city centre. But they also helped change its economic performance and prospects, and the way it did business. They were critical to the renaissance of Liverpool. They are the next part of our story.

Liverpool Vision – the city centre takes off

Liverpool Vision, the city centre's urban regeneration company, was another public-sector intervention that played a critical part in the jigsaw of the Liverpool

renaissance.[6] Urban Regeneration Companies (URCs) were introduced by the Labour government in response to the Richard Rogers Task Force report in 1999.[7] They were different from previous models, especially the Urban Development Corporations, which had had substantial budgets and extensive planning powers. URCs were not intended to undertake development directly but to work in partnership, maximising the powers and expertise of existing agencies. They were set up where local partners wanted them, rather than being imposed by government. They got no separate resources or specific powers and relied on existing agencies for their core funding.[8] The URC model was everything the city had not been in the past. URCs were to be partnership-based. Although publicly initiated, they were to be market-facing, business-friendly, private-sector oriented and led. They were to be mean and lean. They were to be voluntary, relying upon influence rather than power. They were to take a long-term strategic view. They were to provide a big picture or vision of where their city was going and a clear plan to deliver it, signed up to by key partners. Creating a successful URC would be a big challenge for Liverpool.

In fact Liverpool Vision was the first URC in the country, set up in 1999 a few weeks before Manchester's – rather to the delight of the locals. Liverpool Vision played a crucial role in transforming the city. Its work and achievements are key to understanding how Liverpool changed itself at the beginning of the twenty-first century. The company was a joint initiative by Liverpool City Council, the Northwest Development Agency and English Partnerships, with the Government Office North West a board observer, a sign of growing trust in Liverpool by government. They brought different people, powers and money to the company – but all brought substantial long-term commitment. The decision to create a dedicated company reflected the recognition that the city centre should be a major driver of economic and social change in the city, but that previous efforts to regenerate it had failed because of a lack of focus and because of the failure to sufficiently engage the private sector.

What challenges did it face?

The challenges of creating a city centre fit for a premier European city were huge. Despite progress in the 1990s, Liverpool was lagging behind many other English cities in its development – but also in its thinking. Having gone through a series of economic, financial and political traumas, it was backward-looking and introspective. The city was still in the headlines for all the wrong reasons. It was not used to working in partnership. Relations between the public and private sector, although improving, were still strained. The legacy of the riots in 1981 hung over community relations. The council's fiscal affairs were in a mess and its services were poor. The impact upon the city centre was visible for everyone to see. It was run down. It was tired. The public realm was neglected. Its shopping had declined and the city had dropped way down the league tables. There was virtually no new investment or building in offices, residential or retail taking place in the city centre. There was not a single crane to be spotted on the skyline. Much of the commercial space was redundant. There had been significant physical improvements in the docklands area through the MDC, but they had not really crossed the road from the docks to the city centre. Despite efforts by a handful of public- and private-sector leaders, the potential of the city centre as an economic driver for Liverpool and its significance in terms of jobs, investment, culture and marketing was not acknowledged. It was regarded as not providing real jobs in real industries. Too often it was seen by local politicians as less important than other parts of Liverpool, because there were no votes there. Nobody was speaking up for the city centre.

But things had begun to change in the city in the mid-1990s. The work of the MDC on the waterfront and the City Challenge initiative on the edge of the city centre, where the major educational and cultural institutions were based, was beginning to pay off. Also a series of local developers, including Beetham, Urban Splash and Neptune Developments, had spotted gaps in the market, seeing the potential of the city's underused assets, and were beginning to do city-centre and edge-of-centre developments. Key players in the city council were beginning to promote the economic opportunity that the city centre presented. So when the government revealed its plans to set up Urban Regeneration Companies, the seeds had already been sown in Liverpool. It helped to crystallise the opportunity, but partners in Liverpool had already decided they had to do something bold and different about the city centre. Liverpool City Council in particular recognised that it had to embrace partnership working.

Making the big plan – the Strategic Regeneration Framework

Liverpool Vision had a small team – at its biggest it amounted to 20 people. Its board consisted of the political and administrative leaders of Liverpool City Council, English Partnerships, the North West Development Agency and invited representatives from the private sector. Its first chair was Joe Dwyer, a Liverpudlian who had made an international career in engineering and construction and had retired to Liverpool. Its key chief executive was Jim Gill, who had helped fix Speke Garston with English Partnerships. Again they were a powerful team. The Liverpool Vision board knew it needed a big plan and commissioned an international consortium to produce one. After extensive public consultation the plan – or Strategic Regeneration Framework – was published in 2000.[9] It was to be the Holy Grail for the next ten years. It set out a series of ambitious, long-term, strategic goals designed to raise the aspiration of a city which for too long had aimed too low and thought too small. The details were less important than the reach of the plan. The big picture was to establish a twenty-first-century economy; improve competitive career prospects; create inclusive communities and a skilled and adaptable workforce; deliver a high-quality, safe urban environment; exploit the city centre's rich historic character; be a benchmark for the next generation of international city centre regeneration; become a world-class tourist destination; become a premier national shopping destination; create a quality lifestyle; improve Liverpool's European image; and bid to become the European Capital of Culture. Some of these ambitions probably could have been endorsed by any city at any time. But the crucial thing was that they were said and signed up to by key partners in Liverpool. They were a major statement of intent.

For the first time also the plan painted a picture of how these big ideas would be translated into action on the ground in the different quarters of the city. They were to transform the Pier Head into a world-class urban environment and strengthen it as a key city centre gateway and visitor destination; create a nurturing business environment and provide the right space for new and existing businesses to flourish; establish linkages within the historic core by creating a mixed-use urban environment and quality public realm; reinforce the Cultural Quarter as a destination and Lime Street station as a quality gateway to the city; create a step-change in Liverpool's retail offer by extending the main retail area of the city centre; develop the King's Dock into a premier leisure and family entertainment facility; and make the Hope Street Quarter a key cultural resource for the city. These aims were broken down into almost 400 specific actions, major and minor.

What did Liverpool Vision achieve?

'Liverpool in 2008 feels very different from a decade ago. The atmosphere then was very negative – even if there was a glimmer of hope. Now it is completely different and there is optimism. Liverpool is becoming successful, even if there is a long way to go. It is not a "no hoper".' – Louise Ellman, MP

When Liverpool Vision ended its work, many key players believed that it had done a good job and that Liverpool had dramatically improved its performance. Did the hard figures bear out their confidence? In fact, they did. There was good news about Liverpool – even though there was further to go. There was even better news about the city centre. It had experienced improvement in population, jobs, education and skill levels, commercial, retail and residential provision, property prices, rental levels and image. It was the productive heart of the city, accounting for more than half of the city's GVA and half of all Liverpool's jobs. And its population had significantly increased. There had been substantial growth in visitors to Liverpool. In 2000 it was the 13th most-visited city by overseas tourists. In 2006 it was the 6th most-visited UK city, with 625,000 international visitors spending £198 million.

The waterfront – the jewel in the crown

Liverpool Vision wanted to make Liverpool a much better destination for visitors, shoppers and business. Creating a world-class waterfront was crucial to that ambition. It was one of its largest and most successful projects. It guided the continuing renaissance of the Golden Triangle of the Liverpool waterfront – the area between the Pier Head, the Arena and Convention Centre and the massive new Liverpool One mixed-use development. This area was the iconic front door to Liverpool. It was also a stage both for people to play on and from which Liverpool projected itself to the outside world. The scale and quality of the developments were impressive. They also showed how the waterfront had weathered the recession better than some other parts of Liverpool, as well some other cities in the UK. In important ways the area was bucking the trend. By the end of the decade the developments completed or in progress in the Golden Triangle included the cruise liner facility; the new Beatles museum; the ferry terminal; the extension of the Leeds–Liverpool canal; the refurbished public realm at the Pier Head; the refurbishment of the Three Graces; the new

Liverpool waterfront, 2007
© McCoy Wynne
(mccoywynne.co.uk)

Liverpool
waterfront, 2017
© McCoy Wynne
(mccoywynne.co.uk)

Museum of Liverpool, the only European museum dedicated to a city's history; the opening of the four-star Hilton hotel; and the Liverpool Conference Centre and Arena.[10]

Creating a business district for Liverpool

Another of Liverpool Vision's major contributions was to help create a real business district in Liverpool city centre. It did not simply focus on building new offices but on place making. Its strategy was to get some quick wins, but then achieve long-term change in the area. The quick wins were City Square, 101 Old Hall Street and the 20 Chapel Street building, to be followed by the place-changing development St Paul's Square by English Cities Fund. The level of developer and investor interest in the area was reflected in the acquisition and refurbishment of existing buildings, notably the Plaza by Bruntwood, Capital Building by Downing Developments and Exchange Flags by UK Land. There was a real increase in developer, investor and occupier confidence. At the end of the decade prime office rents were up and yields were in line with many of the UK's strongest performing cities. Demand for quality office space had been strong. The crunch affected the city but the percentage of empty office space in the central business district barely changed, when it might have been expected to increase sharply. Take-up of office space by creative, media and IT businesses and Grade A office space flourished.

Increasing living and staying in the city centre

Living in the city centre was transformed as Liverpool Vision planned. In 2000 there was barely a housing market in the city centre beyond the waterfront. That dramatically changed with massive increases in provision. In 1991 only 2,300 people lived in the core area. By 2010 over 23,000 lived there, about 40% of whom were students. The city centre's hotel offer had improved enormously. Leading international chains and new boutique hotels had invested in the city centre. In 2000 there were 17 hotels in the city centre offering 2,000 rooms. By 2010 there were 40 hotels and over 4,000 rooms built or ready for completion by the end of the year. Over 40% of the hotels were four-star, and several more were under construction or planned for the city centre. Occupancy rates had also improved from 68% in 2004 to 75% in 2008.

Attracting shopping and leisure fit for Scousers – Liverpool One

'The Liverpool One Masterplan has single handedly reversed the fortunes of the city by bringing a new social and economic vibrancy to what was 42 acres of historic but derelict buildings at its heart.' – The Stirling Prize Nomination 2009

The quality of shopping dramatically improved in the city centre during the decade. The key development was Grosvenor Estates' development Liverpool One.[11] This massive development extended the existing main retail area and linked the waterfront to the retail and cultural quarter. The existence of Liverpool Vision did not make Grosvenor think of Liverpool in the first instance, but it encouraged it to stay with the idea. The project was desperately needed. Despite the regeneration work done in Albert Dock, the city centre remained blighted. The Albert Dock development was cut off from the rest of the city centre. The city centre was also pockmarked with swathes of underutilised land, with empty lots being used as vast car parks. Liverpool's shopping offer and infrastructure, such as St John's precinct and Paradise Street bus station, was ageing and being increasingly outperformed by out-of-town shopping. Liverpool One transformed this.[12] The 42-acre site cost over £1.4 billion, involving 234,000 sq. metres of total development. 154,000 sq. metres of retail space opened in 2008, including major new stores for John Lewis and Debenhams. It created 21,500 sq. metres of leisure facilities, over 600 residential units, two hotels and 2.2 hectares of open space. The project created over 4,400 permanent jobs on top of 3,300 construction jobs. Liverpool One was a massive success – arguably one of the best mixed-use developments in western Europe. It offered a huge range of shopping and leisure activities around a handsome park. It attracted enormous interest for the quality of its architecture and public realm. It was a commercial success also. It attracted huge numbers of visitors – 20 million shopped there in the first year. It moved Liverpool up from 17th to 5th in the national retail league table. The residential lynchpin of Liverpool One was One Park West, a major development designed

by Caesar Pelli, but it was essentially the quality of the development that stood out. The architecture and public realm raised the bar far higher for Liverpool than ever before.

Raising quality

Liverpool Vision treated place quality as a crucial economic intervention – not a luxury item – which was critical to attracting and retaining talent, clients and investors in the sunrise industries. By the end of the decade the quality of the developments in shops, apartments, office space, hotels, and leisure and conference facilities in the area had raised Liverpool's national and international offer and visibility. For the first time in many years good modern architecture had been added to a city that had had a lot of experience of regenerating Georgian and Victorian architecture but rather less of producing new buildings that matched its historic inheritance. The developments physically expanded and reshaped the city centre in a remarkably short time. They brought the city centre downtown to the waterfront. In the process they revitalised the existing tourist and leisure facilities at Albert Dock. And this created demand for higher-quality services and facilities in the whole area. So the economic value and potential of the whole area was lifted. But none of this was guaranteed at the start of the decade. The speed as well as the scale and quality of the changes that took place surprised many – especially those accustomed to the way things happened in old Liverpool.

Changing the city's mood music

Liverpool and the city centre came a very long way in a very short time. Liverpool Vision contributed enormously to that. Two decades of economic and political challenges had undermined Liverpool's performance and prospects and had created a culture of failure. So as important as the economic and physical changes that took place were the changes in spirit and mood in the city during this decade. Liverpool became more ambitious, more confident, more market-oriented. The private sector saw Liverpool as a place to invest and make money. Partners worked together better. The city was developing a track record for delivery – of being a 'can do' rather than a 'can't do' place. The different quarters and activities of the city were much better connected. The city centre looked and felt like a more coherent place. In the past, economic and political challenges had undermined Liverpool's performance and created a culture of low ambition. But big improvements in the city centre had changed the way that people inside and outside the city saw Liverpool. Liverpool Vision was crucial to that.

'Liverpool Vision was the factor that got us to be serious about Liverpool.' – Rod Holmes, Grosvenor Estates, Liverpool One

In fact, Rod Holmes, the project director, was himself crucial. He was the moving force on the ground for Liverpool One and the person who ensured that it was a living place that reflected the history of the city and respected the views of public and voluntary groups.

What were the secrets of success?

Before Liverpool Vision, the city centre was not a priority for the city council. Essentially it did patch and mend – and it showed. Liverpool Vision made a big plan for the city centre that required strategic rather than reactive thinking.

It gave a theme around which players could mobilise and a clear route map for the city centre. That simple statement increased investor and developer confidence. It brought money into Liverpool. Liverpool City Council was financially constrained and had many competing demands on its resources. Liverpool Vision actively lobbied public partners for the city centre and made sure that substantial additional money came into Liverpool. It persuaded the North West Development Agency that Liverpool city centre was important and that Liverpool Vision could deliver programmes. It got the trust of the agency in a way that the local authority might not have done. It also mobilised European Union money. It persuaded the Objective 1 committee to create a special financial measure of £50 million for the waterfront in addition to the city centre measure. Getting these commitments gave symbolic as well as financial support for the centre.

Liverpool Vision built bridges between the public and private sectors. Cities need the private sector to invest, but often local authorities do not have the attitudes or skills to attract this. They are often not business-friendly enough. Liverpool Vision had no such inhibitions. It promoted the interests of the developer to the local authority, which gave developers confidence. But it did not compromise the local authority. By acting as the private face of the public sector, Liverpool Vision helped the private sector to see Liverpool as a place in which it could do business. When Liverpool Vision started, no development took place in Liverpool without a grant. When it ended, this had changed. It had the right people at the right time in the right place. Regeneration agencies are as good as the people in them – and as good as the relationships they make with key partners. Liverpool Vision passed this test. It had a well-regarded chair who could reassure the private sector but not threaten people. It had a powerful board with senior private-sector players who remained committed and involved throughout. It had a chief executive who knew both the private- and public-sector worlds and could speak to both. It had a team brought from and with very good contacts to the major public partners – the local authority, Northwest Development Agency and English Partnerships.

Liverpool Vision stayed committed to its core business. It focused on the city centre. It focused on physical development. It showed that the centre was crucial to the city's economic prospects and persuaded the city council to support it. Regenerating the city centre was not always as important to elected members as education, social services and housing, which might matter more to their ward voters. Vision made and won the argument that the city centre mattered. It also succeeded because it had a big plan that the partners understood, bought into and supported. It got the public onside. Vision got the private sector onside and helped make the local authority more business-friendly. It flourished because it had a degree of independence from its public-sector funders. But Vision's greatest achievement and the secret of its success was that it built trust between all the partners. And that helped change Liverpool.

It was not perfect

There were two big projects that Liverpool Vision put forward that it was unable to deliver. The first was a proposed Fourth Grace called the Cloud at the Pier Head, to be delivered by the leading architect Will Alsop. The second was a light rapid Merseytram which would loop around the city centre and then beyond. Both were ambitious if controversial projects which were abandoned. They were visible and controversial failures and at the time raised questions about the city's ability to deliver big projects. There had not been enough clarity at the outset about the real purpose of the Cloud, and it was abandoned in less than ideal circumstances. They also underlined the point that, despite the progress it was making, there remained questions about the extent of political consensus and mature leadership in the city as well as the technical capacity to deliver major projects. But the city leaders survived the travails and learned from them. It did not stop them delivering many other successful projects then and later. In fact it could be argued that the Cloud was probably best not delivered. The Pier Head site at Mann Island was subsequently filled by an innovative black glass building, though that project remains controversial for some. The tram, however, was and remains a miss, as the success of Manchester's tram experience demonstrates. But the path to success is usually littered with obstacles and failures. The key is how a place and its leaders respond to them. Liverpool's did and have.

Other city centre initiatives helped Liverpool Vision

The work of Liverpool Vision was aided and abetted by the work of two other external bodies. The Local Strategic Partnership (LSP), again a nationally inspired government initiative, was a parallel city-wide partnership that grew out of the team originally set up to administer the Objective 1 programme and coordinate the efforts of the major players with a stake in the city. It produced a ten-year regeneration strategy across all agencies at the local authority level. This complemented the strategic ambitions of Liverpool Vision, arguing that the city centre should become the magnet for commercial investment, residential expansion, leisure and tourism and develop its key role in the future economic growth of the region. The LSP influenced the second European Objective 1 programme to give £38 million for city centre redevelopment. Liverpool also used another national initiative, the Single Regeneration Budget (SRB), to develop the city centre.[13] This Cityfocus SRB recognised the opportunity in the city centre but also the challenges it faced. It had lost office space and had little quality. It did not have a business park. Retail space was in short supply and there were not enough multiple retailers. The environment was poor, with little greenery and open space. The streetscape was cluttered. Traffic dominated the centre but was inefficient. There were a lot of vacant and derelict buildings. It focused on three broad areas: the Cultural Quarter and Lime Street, the connecting area of Castle Street/Exchange Flags and the Pier Head and waterfront.

These programmes made a huge difference to the city centre, as Hilary Russell's review demonstrated. The £25 million SRB and £38 million ERDF attracted £95 million of private and over £100 million of public-sector funding. It created over 1,000 jobs and protected another 1,000, and attracted £35 million of investment into the city centre. In 1997 employment Liverpool in the city centre was 89,000, in 2000 97,000, and by 2006 it was 112,000. It grew faster than the rest of the city, the surrounding local authorities and the nation. GVA went up by £200 million to £250 million between 2000 and 2004. In 1998 the GVA per head of population in Liverpool was 14.6% lower than the UK average. By 2005, it was only 10.3% lower. Total visitor spend rose from £261 million in 2000 to £424 million in 2006.

These programmes and money contributed to the delivery of the Liverpool One development by Grosvenor. They improved the physical environment of the retail area. They encouraged the development of the Metquarter. They supported the King's Waterfront development with the Arena and Convention Centre. They supported the cruise liner terminal and the refurbishment of the Bluecoat arts centre. Hotel provision was dramatically increased and overnight visitors doubled from 800,000 in 2000 to 1.6 million in 2006. The commercial office market changed during these years. Uptake by private-sector firms increased. Grade A rental increased from £16 per sq. ft in 2003 to £18 in 2005, £20 in 2006 and £21 in 2007. Between 2000 and 2006, city centre office rents increased by 40% compared with a 34% average increase in other Core Cities. Between 1996 and 2005, 4,514 residential units were built and 8,132 student bedspaces. The combination of money, people and capacity from the overlapping initiatives of Liverpool Vision, Cityfocus SRB and European programmes and the Local Strategic Partnership all fuelled the continuing renaissance of Liverpool city centre.

'There was great collaboration between the strategic funders and planners. The sense of joint purpose and working was much greater than in other places I had worked in.' – Professor Michael Brown

Capital of Culture – a second jewel in the crown

'The capital of culture bid was nothing short of an act of faith, underpinned largely by a glorious but not necessarily fully developed or enabled vision of a city that could take on such large scale challenges.' – Liverpool city councillor[14]

The crucial single event that really changed Liverpool's performance, prospects and image at this time was winning in 2003 and delivering in 2008 the European Capital of Culture. It dramatically changed the city's ability to deliver major projects. It increased external and internal confidence and later investment. It raised its profile with politicians and the media. It was the beginning of a new phase of Liverpool's creativity and culture. It changed everything about the city, as Beatriz Garcia's assessment underlined.[15]

The original idea of trying to win the Capital of Culture came from the consultants commissioned to prepare the Strategic Regeneration Plan by Liverpool Vision. Bob Scott, who had led Manchester's failed Olympic bids but its successful Commonwealth Games bid, was the driving force behind it. The UK government was given the responsibility for deciding which UK city would be the European Capital of Culture. Bidding by 12 cities started in 2000 and the government gave the title to Liverpool in June 2003. It marked a key shift in public perceptions of Liverpool from a city of confrontation and chaos to a city with genuine European ambitions and aspirations. Regenerating the city centre and repositioning the city was at the core of its bid. It played to many of the city's strengths – its revitalised city centre, its history of creativity, storytelling and theatre, as well its wider cultural achievements and ambitions. But it was a huge surprise to many in the city when the bid won. As one city councillor put it:

Just bidding was a Liverpool success story. The fact we were able to put in what most agreed was a courageous and serious bid was a sign of growing confidence and ambition. For somewhere that only a few years ago was typically held to be the benchmark for poverty of ambition this really has been a miracle.[16]

Capital of Culture official opening ceremony
Image reproduced by permission of Culture Liverpool, Liverpool City Council

In 2000 the Liverpool Culture Company was created to prepare and eventually deliver the bid. It had 100 staff, of whom half were new appointments and the other half were secondments from the city council. There were also secondments from a range of organisations across the city. A board of 28 city-wide representatives ran the organisation. But the board was unwieldy and was cut down to seven as 2008 approached. The governance of the project was complex and went through some ups and downs because of this. But the extent of the stakeholder involvement and the number of partnerships formed outweighed the operational challenges it created.

It worked – culturally, financially and politically

'Capital of Culture was a chance for the city to come together. It was something we could tell a story about. It brought the whole world into one city. It brought the pride back to the place.' – Claire McColgan

Capital of Culture was intended to reposition Liverpool with national and international audiences, increase local communities' participation in cultural activities, leave a legacy for the city and promote the role of the arts and

culture in regenerating UK cities. The programme spanned several years before the main event in 2008, with different themes in each year. It was a commercial, cultural, political and policy success, as Garcia's work again showed. Culturally, it presented a wide range of events showcasing local, national and international talent and acclaimed work. It reached a variety of audiences and got lots of local engagement from different social classes. It was a financial success. It created work and income. Artists provided over 123,000 days' work over the whole period, 50% of them locally based. The company spent £130 million over the four years, slightly over half provided by the city council. It earned £21 million in sponsorship and generated £4 million income. The audience over the four years was 18 million: 60% came from the city region, 15% from the north-west, 20% were national and 5% were international. Over 60% of the audiences judged 2008 as very good. The seven existing major cultural attractions in Liverpool increased their attendance by over 50%.

It was a reputational success. Businesses reported improved perceptions of the city as well as increased turnover. It increased the numbers of visitors to the city – 35% of visitors in 2008 came because of the title. Many came for the first time. Over 2 million stayed overnight. They spent over £600 million. The event increased the supply of hotels, which were over 85% full during the year. Media coverage of Liverpool increased and improved in tone. Peer perceptions improved and in 2009 over half of arts organisations, funders, promoters and key national figures agreed that Liverpool had achieved its ambition to reposition itself as a world-class city. National awareness of Liverpool increased so that in 2008 over 60% of the UK population knew about its role. During the four years running up to 2008 national perceptions of the city improved, with positive views of Liverpool nationally increasing from 53% to 60%. Visitor satisfaction with Liverpool also increased. Local opinion of the city improved as the numbers of residents believing that Liverpool was better than other cities for hotels, music, galleries and shopping increased significantly between 2005 and 2008. Local residents' views of the city were also improved. Significant majorities thought the event would bring increased investment, make the place better, attract new jobs and would bring benefits to all parts of the city. Key players believed it had helped deliver important physical and cultural infrastructure to the city. It had helped alleviate the impact of the economic downturn. In particular the delivery of Liverpool One and the Echo Arena and Convention Centre in time for 2008 were crucial associated impacts of the year.

'It was a turning point. The fact that it could organise itself was a major step. But more than that, the delivery was a defining moment – living proof that Liverpool had changed and could deliver.' – Robert Hough

Capital of Culture was a crucial landmark in Liverpool's continuing renaissance. It brought both tangible and symbolic benefits and played a critical role in

La Machine, 2008
Image reproduced by permission of Culture Liverpool, Liverpool City Council

repositioning the city. It moved Liverpool on – culturally, economically, physically and politically. It showed that the city could deliver an international event of quality and class. It reshaped the city centre and added to its visitor infrastructure. It strengthened partnership working and civic leadership. It raised local aspirations and ambitions. It created internal and external confidence – with both investors and government. And it was victory snatched from the jaws of potential defeat. Few involved thought they would win the competition. The year before it was delivered there were wobbles and worries. At one point the company lost its high-profile Australian chief executive. But those apprehensions were ended by its chair Phil Redmond's insistence on national radio that it would be a Scouse wedding – in prospect chaotic but in practice a fantastic, warm-hearted, if occasionally rumbustious affair. With it Liverpool turned another proverbial corner. The city and its key organisations delivered. Both they and outsiders knew it could do it again. 2008 was a good year but its significance was far greater. Liverpool had come of age again.[17]

How far had the aspiring premier European city come by 2010?

It was clear in 2010 that Liverpool had had a very good decade. It had built upon the normalisation that had begun in the 1990s and seized the opportunity presented by New Labour's expansive approach to public expenditure and commitment to cities, as well as the private sector's realisation that cities were extremely good market places with the potential to deliver on investment. Liverpool Vision had been the precipitator of many of the changed ambitions, attitudes and actions. Government programmes such as SRB and the revised approach by the city council provided a fertile context for its work. European money had continued to give. Capital of Culture was the icing on the cake, giving the city a brilliant showcase for what it was good at – partying in style.

The politics in the city were much better. The city council was changing its performance, attitudes and behaviour. There had been an enormous amount of high-quality investment in the city centre and the waterfront. The bar had been raised in terms of the quality of the shopping, leisure and cultural offer. The architectural and physical environment in which they had been placed was high. And the jewel in the crown of the waterfront continued to flourish, again partly because of the high quality of the developments there. There had been a step-change in attitude, ambition and achievement in Liverpool. It continued to face many challenges, but the best of what it achieved in the city centre was unimaginable a decade earlier. And it had happened incredibly quickly.

Stirred but not shaken by austerity

Even though it was clear that the next years would be more difficult, Liverpool had not been crippled by the economic troubles. By 2010 the city had come a long way in a short time. The city centre had come further. But the challenges ahead were big. The journey was just beginning. The national and international economy would not be as buoyant. There would be much less public money. Much development that had been planned might not happen. After 2008 austerity had been difficult for regeneration projects and city centre developments right across the country. Liverpool was lucky since much of its regeneration was completed or had been long planned, before the crunch hit too deeply. If the crisis had happened three years earlier, many of its big developments would not have been completed. But they had been. Crucially many of the things that were planned for the area in 2008 continued. It meant that Liverpool had begun to build critical mass of real quality in a crucial area of the city. It also helped to sustain momentum at a time when development in other parts of the city had slowed down.

Notes

1   Michael Parkinson, 'Scoring Goals and Back in the Premier League', in *Parliamentary Brief: Liverpool City Report* (July 2001).

2   David Robertson, 'The Two Men Who Have to Tiptoe across the Eggshells', in *Parliamentary Brief: Liverpool City Report* (July 2001).

3   Cocks, op. cit., p. 233.

4   Eileen Milner and Paul Joyce, *Lessons in Leadership* (Routledge, 2005).

5   Liverpool City Council, *A Ten Year Prospectus for a Distinct European City* (2003).

6   Parkinson, *Make No Little Plans* (Liverpool Vision, 2008).

7   Richard Rogers, *Towards an Urban Renaissance* (DETR, 1999).

8   Michael Parkinson and Brian Robson, *Urban Regeneration Companies: A Process Evaluation* (HMSO, DETR 2000).

9   Skidmore, Owings and Merrill, *Strategic Regeneration Framework* (Liverpool Vision, 2000).

10 Michael Parkinson, *Liverpool City Centre: Maintaining Momentum, Raising Quality*, report to Grosvenor Estates and Neptune Developments (2010).

11 Alex Nurse, 'City Regeneration to Drive Economic Competitiveness: The Case Study of Liverpool One', *LHI Journal*, 8.2 (2017).

12 David Littlefield (ed.), *Liverpool One: Remaking a City Centre* (Wiley, 2009).

13 Hilary Russell, *City Focus Strategic Review* (European Institute for Urban Affairs, LJMU, 2007).

14 Quoted in Milner and Joyce, op. cit., p. 104.

15 Beatriz Garcia et al., *Creating an Impact: Liverpool's Experience as European Capital of Culture* (University of Liverpool: Impact 08, 2010).

16 Quoted in Milner and Joyce, op. cit., p. 109.

17 Philip Boland, 'Capital of Culture – You Must be Having a Laugh. A Critical Appraisal of Liverpool 08', *Social and Cultural Geography*, 11.7 (2010), presents a rather more sceptical view of the programme.

CHAPTER FIVE

Continuing ambition in an age of austerity, 2010–19

Liverpool had a very good boom during the first decade of the twenty-first century. It improved its own economic performance and closed the gap on some other UK cities. But even though the city also had a relatively decent bust, austerity and the policies of the Coalition and subsequently the Conservative government had an impact. In fact, in 2010 Liverpool again underlined the peculiarities of its politics when, just as in 1998, city voters threw out of office the party that had just done very well in the national elections. Liverpool returned decisively to Labour in 2010. The subsequent period was marked by three features. The first was the creation in 2012 of the office of an elected mayor in Liverpool. The second was austerity, with a Labour council increasingly hit by cuts in national government resources trying to sustain the economic development of the city that had taken place in the golden age. During this time the Labour leadership and the mayor had to straddle two different horses – trying to maintain economic development while at the same time carrying out the government's austerity programme, which hit hardest the poorest people in the poorest parts of the city. And they were attempting to do so without losing political support in the city or returning to the failed 1980s politics of confrontation. The third feature of this period was devolution and the move by national government to give responsibilities, if not always resources, to local government, with a raft of institutional changes including City Deals and elected city and later city regional mayors and Combined Authorities. This move changed and challenged the face of decision making in Liverpool as in other British cities. This chapter looks at the way in which those forces played out. It does three things. It assesses the performance and impact of Liverpool's elected mayor as he tried to sustain economic development with a commitment to pragmatic rather than gesture politics. It judges how the move to city regional government, including the election of a city regional mayor, worked out in Liverpool. And it assesses the impact of austerity and cuts in government resources to local councils on the city's finances and capacity.

Liverpool's elected mayor – did he add value and encourage Liverpool's renaissance?

Liverpool was the first big city outside London to adopt the elected city mayor model, which both Labour and Conservative governments had been promoting for several years, but which had been rejected by voters in a number of cities in referenda. In 2012 as part of a major deal with the Coalition government, the Labour-controlled city council decided to adopt an elected mayor model of government without holding a referendum. The leader of the Labour council, Joe Anderson, was elected by the Liverpool voters in 2012 for four years with a significant majority. He was re-elected for a further four years in 2016. The office of elected mayor was controversial in a number of cities and it was a leap in the dark for Liverpool. It was another important experiment in a city that had had more urban experiments than any other UK city. An elected mayor was intended to be very different from a traditional council leader. The role was supposed to be more visible, more accountable, more powerful and more effective. The key question was would an elected mayor be better than a traditional leader and make a difference to Liverpool's economic performance and prospects? I tried to answer that question in 2016.[1]

In fact, the idea of an elected mayor was not without opposition in the city at the start. Some people did not want it. Some thought the mayor would not have the powers and resources to deliver. Some thought Liverpool's traditional political challenges would stop the experiment from working. Some were worried about the concentration of power and limited accountability of the mayor. The shadow of the previous Militant regime with its bossism and cronyism always hung over the office and the mayor, however unfairly. But despite reservations in some quarters, there was also a lot of support for the idea among senior decision makers in the private as well as public sectors in the city. In fact, many of their expectations were very high. For example, many believed that the city was not sufficiently prominent on the radar of the private sector, international markets, the media or national government. They thought an elected mayor would cause Liverpool to be seen and heard more in high places at home and abroad.

Equally, in their view Liverpool had suffered from a lack of clear, coherent, decisive leadership in the past. A mayor was expected to provide a single voice for the city and a clearer economic narrative about its future that could unite different partners, sectors and organisations. A mayor was expected to raise the tone and level of the debate beyond partisan politics and focus on the long-term interests of the city rather than those of his own political party. Key players also hoped that a mayor would improve the efficiency and effectiveness of the council, making it more innovative, quicker in its decision making and better at delivery. Since an elected mayor was effectively a condition of the freedoms and resources that Liverpool got from its City Deal with government in 2012, people expected that an elected mayor would improve Liverpool's relationship with national government. Although the relationship had been improving in the recent past, there was a view that a mayor would help bridge that historic gap and perhaps get easier access to and more money from government. Whichever way it was looked at, there were a lot of expectations riding on Liverpool's elected mayor experiment. Could the office deliver?

What difference did a mayor make?

When first elected in 2012, Anderson promised to build new schools, create new jobs and create new homes. In fact, he did achieve his major quantitative targets during his first four years in office. He spent £170 million on a capital investment programme, created 2,000 construction jobs and built 12 new schools. He delivered 5,000 new homes – two-thirds for sale, one-third for social or affordable rent. He met his 20,000 jobs pledge. But while these quantitative targets mattered, the key question and expectation was about the mayor's use of soft power. And here many senior players, especially in the private sector, thought that the elected mayor had been a success. They believed he had shown leadership nationally and internationally. He had a bigger agenda than a traditional council leader. He could do things more quickly and deal well with external partners and the private sector. Many key players were more optimistic about Liverpool and thought its profile was much higher – and they gave the mayor some of the credit for that. There was considerable admiration for his commitment, passion, enthusiasm and self-deprecating style. He wore his heart on his sleeve to defend both the city and its people. He was regarded by many – although not all – as a genuine Scouser pursuing the city's rather than his personal interests.

Because of and despite austerity, the mayor and his office showed a lot of commitment and success in exploring ways of raising money in difficult times. His office was active in trying to develop more systematic ways of mobilising and packaging sources of funding, as opposed to simply chasing individual pots. It developed the Mayoral Investment Fund, through which the authority used either its own assets, its ability to borrow at historically low levels or available grant to invest in local growth. It developed and funded a number of projects, including extending the Convention Centre with an Exhibition Centre, purchasing its own offices in the Cunard building, buying a city centre site freehold to allow the construction of a hotel, and supporting a very successful high-tech manufacturing company. It won the Municipal Journal's Award for Innovation in Finance in 2016. The Capital of Culture had been an important driver in Liverpool's renaissance. The mayor kept that strategy going by retaining and paying for the cultural team to deliver prestige events and projects that attracted people, attention and investment to the city. A crucial example was the International Festival for Business, which was part of the 2012 City Deal with national government. It was successfully delivered in 2014 and was repeated with government support in 2016, and with support from the city region's Strategic Investment Fund in 2018. Forcefully driven by the high-profile chief executive of Liverpool Vision, Max Steinberg, IFB brought international visitors and investment, and it enhanced Liverpool's reputation and profile as a place where national and international business could invest. The culture team, led by Claire McColgan, encouraged the attraction of the major Festivals of the Giants, which were cultural and financial successes in 2012, 2014 and 2018. The Three Queens event when Cunard's three ocean liners visited the city in 2015 brought similar attention and money to Liverpool, with one million people lining the Mersey to see their appearance, generating £30 million in economic impact. In different ways these 'soft' projects raised the city's profile, visibility, reputation and income.

'Joe played a pioneering role in delivering devolution in this country. He was the first of the big city leaders to seize the opportunity of an elected mayor.' – Lord Michael Heseltine

The mayor was crucial in getting devolved powers and money to Liverpool city region. He encouraged local politicians to sign up for the agenda and persuaded government that Liverpool city region could be trusted to deliver a devolution deal. However, constructing a consensus in the city region was not easy. There were tensions between the local authorities, their elected leaders and private-sector partners. Such tensions were not unusual in cities that were coming to terms with new working relationships and models that presented cultural challenges. Liverpool was probably no worse than some other city regions. But the effort to build agreement consumed a lot of the mayor's time and energy. If relationships had already been more collaborative, he would have had more time and energy to focus on the city of Liverpool's affairs.

The mayor managed to increase the city's profile with, access to and potential influence over government. As one civil servant put it, 'We see Liverpool differently because it has a Mayor. It looks different to us than other cities. We know we can trust him.' The original City Deal brought extra powers and resources to the city. For example, government made an exception about closing the Labour government's Building Schools for the Future programme and gave Liverpool the money needed to deliver it. It brought a range of institutional initiatives including a Mayoral Development Corporation and Development Zones. Some players argued that the mayor did not succeed in attracting extra resources to the city because its basic budget was so severely cut. But austerity was a national government strategy and no individual city could have avoided significant cuts. Also the cuts began before he had done his devolution deal with

the government in 2012. Nevertheless, the fiscal stresses on the city were and remain a crucial issue for the future, as we shall see later.

But not perfect

Anderson delivered a series of important initiatives. The role suited his style and personality. But there were constraints and limits on his performance. For example, many wanted a clearer longer-term economic narrative for the city, which identified its underlying assets and long-term ambitions in a well-argued case. The mayor was good at responding to problems and crises but less good at addressing systematically the longer-term issues facing their sectors. There were also some concerns about the extent of the mayor's accountability to voters and the city council. Some thought he was closer to developers than industrialists. Some thought he was too close to the daily operations of the council. Some argued that his office was not big enough and did not have enough of the right skills and experience.

However, the mayor's biggest constraint was austerity. He was in the invidious position of wanting to cooperate with government on devolution and the city regional agenda but at the same time having to manage significant cuts in national government resources to Liverpool. It gave him, the city council and its officers a huge challenge. He had to walk a tightrope between making clear that the scale of the cuts was anathema to him, but not returning to the failed policies of the 1980s and threatening protests or even bankruptcy. Austerity drained both his resources and capacity. It meant that the city council lost senior people just as the mayoral initiative was being created. Too much of the mayor's time and energy and that of his remaining senior staff was spent on managing austerity rather than focusing upon longer-term strategic issues. Those were sacrificed in the drive to manage daily crises and challenges. More importantly, austerity meant that there was simply less money to be innovative or even to deliver desirable projects. Anderson did a good job in that politically tricky area. He himself argued that simply keeping the city council show on the road was his most significant achievement – far greater than his soft power achievements or prestige projects. 'I am most proud of the fact I have been able to promote and champion the city through austerity. It is my biggest achievement. It may not be sexy like the Giants. But to have managed the cuts and still promote the city gives me a huge sense of pride.'

The balance sheet on an elected mayor in Liverpool

A continuing concern about Liverpool since its trials and tribulations in the 1980s has been its ability to manage services efficiently, work in partnership with the private sector, provide clear leadership for the city and build good relationships with national government. Did the elected mayor experiment do anything to improve its performance? The view of many senior decision makers nationally and locally is that it did. There were limits, as we have seen. Austerity limited his achievements. Also the economic challenges of Liverpool are structural and could not be eliminated by a single institutional initiative. The personality and style of the mayor often divided opinion, creating opponents as well as supporters. The role of the city mayor was also affected by the creation in 2017 of an elected city regional mayor. Nevertheless, the experiment was a success. Liverpool made the office work. It delivered some tangible and potential economic benefits. It provided clearer leadership, engaged the private sector, built links with government and raised the profile of the city nationally and internationally. The city council continued to face challenges in terms of capacity and delivery. Nevertheless, the elected mayor was an important factor in reconstructing the political capacity of the broken post-imperial city.

'The council functions better. Joe has worked with the private sector. The government takes us seriously. Joe has opposed the cuts but not had a go at government when he doesn't need to. He has had bad cuts but has not had thousands in the streets protesting.' – Dame Louise Ellman, MP

Scaling up – from the city of Liverpool to Liverpool city region

The main focus of this book has been the performance and continuing renaissance of the city of Liverpool. But the next section widens its focus to the larger territory of Liverpool city region. This is important since in recent years, and especially since the devolution deal of 2016, political attention in the UK has increasingly focused upon city regions as part of a more general policy debate about the best way of running UK cities to improve the performance of the national economy. I discuss these wider policy issues next before looking at Liverpool in detail.

The performance of cities and city regions is crucial to national economic performance. Much European evidence shows that countries that have high-performing cities beyond the capital city also have higher-performing and better-balanced economies. By contrast, those that keep their economic eggs in one basket tend to underperform or are at potential risk. The UK, because of the institutional, economic and financial dominance of London, is one of the latter. However, national government has recognised this reality and is, if belatedly and slowly, moving in the other direction. It is moving some responsibilities and powers – if not yet enough resources – out of Whitehall and Westminster into the local hands of those whose economic fate and futures are directly at stake. It is also moving to a different form of governance where decisions are taken at the level of the functional urban economy – the city region – rather than at narrow local government boundaries. This is crucial. Local authorities are simply too small to operate successfully in a rapidly changing global economy. At present, the UK has nineteenth-century government based on twentieth-century boundaries to manage a twenty-first-century economy.[2]

This agenda challenged many city regional leaders across England. Governing at a wider city regional rather than a local authority level presented cultural challenges. Local authority leaders were asked to do new things in new ways at the same time as having to accept big cuts in their budgets. And the government's belief in market forces and a radically reduced state sector presented particular challenges in city regions where the market was weaker and where public-sector intervention to encourage private investment remained important to economic performance. But the local politics of turf are also difficult, with several barriers to progress. There is often a lack of vision, where key players simply do not see the economic and social opportunities that operating at a bigger scale can bring. There can be fragmentation when too many institutions and strategies operate in the same space and don't see the need for rationalisation. Often there are historic tensions between places, where memories of previous differences and conflicts prevent recognition of a greater shared identity or destiny. There can be personal rivalries as elected leaders pursue their individual self-interest at the expense of collaboration for the greater common good. Also there are party rivalries, where different parts of the territory are controlled by different political parties or where there are shifting patterns of allegiance. And there can be complacency about the area's prospects, where people think the current performance is good enough and don't see the risks of global economic change and the need to plan and respond to them at a wider territorial level. At the heart of the argument there are often economic rivalries, where places in the same space compete for public and private investment at the expense of the surrounding communities. Liverpool, like many other city regions in the UK, continues to face some of those dilemmas.

Tackling these barriers is complex. The evidence from Europe is that the larger city must not bully smaller places. There has to be trust that all places will benefit and none will be exploited. Incentives from national governments can encourage collaboration. Successful city regions have a degree of self-confidence gained from a track record of delivering their strategic ambitions. They build vision, strategy, partnership leadership and trust. They generate political support for a plan. They build organisational capacity. They understand that it is not a quick fix and stick at it long term. Crucially, successful city regions have mature politics and strategic leadership.

How did the national city regional agenda play out in Liverpool?

The real impact of these policy changes hit Liverpool in 2016 when the six local authorities that make up Liverpool city region made a devolution deal with government in which a Combined Authority and an elected city regional mayor were given powers that could affect the city region's future economic performance. They were given a degree of responsibility for skills, employment, housing, planning, transport, innovation, business growth and support, energy and environment, culture and European funding. The Combined Authority also got some new fiscal powers with the creation of a Single Investment Fund, which combined in a single pot a range of existing city regional and national funds. Government promised to top up those funds with a contribution of £30 million annually for thirty years.

In fact a first issue that the Liverpool leaders had to address was a crucial economic but also highly political one – where were the city region's real boundaries? Local authority boundaries increasingly make little sense in a globalised economy. Decisions have to be taken on wider boundaries that more accurately reflect the real functional economy rather than the narrower administrative boundaries of the local authority, which are too small to deliver urban economic success. This raised the question whether Liverpool city region was really a single economic entity or a collection of six separate local authorities. In fact the evidence about where people live, work and what they earn underlined that it was an integrated economy in which the different local authority areas were connected and had an important impact on each other, as the *The State of Liverpool City Region Report* (SOLCRR) showed.[3] Working at city regional level made simple economic sense for Liverpool. People in all six local authorities moved across boundaries to work. Liverpool was a key source of jobs for the wider city region. More workers commuted into it than went in the opposite direction. But it was a symbiotic relationship. The city fed the city region workforce, but the city's firms needed inward commuters. And the other districts needed the city's workplaces for jobs. In addition, Liverpool city region was not hermetically sealed. Many of its residents worked outside it and many people who lived outside Liverpool city region travelled to work in it. So the natural economy was even bigger than the one captured by the city region boundaries. The different economic strengths of the city region – advanced manufacturing, logistics, health and life sciences, computing, tourism – were found across the city region. The different parts of the city region were connected economically and they needed to collaborate politically.

So operating successfully at a city regional level would be one of the keys to the future success of Liverpool. However, building identity, collaboration and trust in a city region is easy to aspire to and difficult to achieve. In fact Liverpool had come some way along the road, as the SOLCRR made clear. Trust was building. Collaborative working was improving. Relationships were more robust and stronger. But the city region had further to go. There was a view that the city region was better at writing strategies than delivering them. The vast majority of partners believed that the city region mattered and supported the principle, but wanted to see greater political commitment. A common identity had not yet been achieved and more hearts and minds had to be won. This would require greater political maturity across the entire city regional leadership class but especially within the local authorities. But progress had been made.

The SOLCRR also underlined that the city region needed to encourage greater collaboration between the public and private sectors and between the different parts of the public sector. There were too many organisations

Commuters
and shoppers,
Queen's Square
bus station,
Liverpool
© Jason Wells/Alamy
Stock Photo

competing in the same space, which created uncertainty in the minds of external investors and government about who spoke for Liverpool city region. There was no single strategy or vision that clearly spelled out the business case for Liverpool and its contribution to the northern and national economy. There were competing messages which, although not necessarily contradictory, were not well aligned. There was no single hymn sheet. Liverpool city regional commitment and confidence was much higher. But in terms of capacity to deliver and commitment to the city region, Liverpool had more to do.

'We have had a decade of pragmatism. We are over rhetoric politics. We have come together and are doing more as a city region. But we are only part way through the journey.' – Mark Basnett, chief executive, LCR Local Enterprise Partnership

A tale of two cities – what messages from Manchester?

To understand the challenges and complexities of city regional working it is worth looking at the experience of Manchester, which has led the debate about city regions in the UK for almost two decades. National government recognised this by giving it the earliest and most expansive devolution deal thus far. There are always sensitivities in Liverpool about discussing Manchester's achievements. Of course, Liverpool must not obsess about its neighbour, because it has wider markets and targets to exploit. But nor should it simply ignore what has happened down the M62. Manchester may be a different place with a different past, economy, geography and leadership model. But mature places are willing to learn from others rather than simply copying them. What are the key messages from Manchester about building a successful city region? They include stability of leadership, building trust between local authorities, making the city region central not peripheral, agreeing upon the importance of the city of Manchester as the regional centre, involving the private sector at the heart of decision making, planning long term, maximising economic assets, winning friends in government, developing a firm evidence base, and investing in city regional capacity, as the SOLCRR again made clear.[4]

Manchester had clear consistent leadership, with only two leaders and effectively two chief executives for over twenty years. It had engaged the private sector in partnership working since the late 1980s. It consistently tried to respond to and even lead national government agendas and win friends in high places. Its leadership had been committed to city regional level partnership working from the late 1990s, building upon, but going beyond, the successful regeneration of Manchester city centre. The leadership of Manchester City Council became less aggressive towards the surrounding local authorities in the city region as it became more confident of its own successes. The destruction of the city centre by an IRA bomb in 1996, when thousands of workers from outside Manchester could not get into work in the city centre, underlined to the other local authority leaders how dependent their own boroughs' economies were on Manchester. It reinforced the need to work together collectively. And the rebuilding of the city centre bound the private sector even further into the decision-making processes about the future of Manchester. The city region was part of the Manchester psyche. It kept the Association of Greater Manchester Authorities together after the abolition of the county council in 1986. And after it achieved its ambition of developing the city centre in the 1990s, it naturally turned to the challenge of making the city region a bigger player.

A key feature in Manchester city region was that all organisations were encouraged to sing from the same hymn sheet. Speakers from Manchester always said the same thing about the city region, its achievements and challenges. It became a mantra that the world eventually believed. They also tried to keep trouble in the family. There were many differences of opinion within Manchester, but its leaders worked hard to keep arguments inside the tent. They were also clear about the need to go with the grain of the market and develop a robust private- rather than public-sector model of the city region. They tried to cultivate good relationships with governments of different persuasions and ask how Manchester could help government deliver its strategic ambitions. And they did long-term thinking. It is said that the former chief executive, Sir Howard Bernstein, wrote the strategy for Manchester in a pamphlet in 1983 where he outlined the significance of the city centre, the universities, the airport and the tram system – and then spent the next thirty years delivering that simple ambition.

The Manchester leaders also worked hard to create a single narrative for the city region. In particular, the Manchester Independent Economic Review in 2007 provided an objective analysis of the opportunities and challenges in the city region, which underlined the need for the local authorities to hang together rather than separately. It became the story that all public- and private-sector partners used. It helped Manchester win allies in government and government money. Manchester continued to invest substantially in its economic and intelligence capacity, supported by all ten local authorities. It was part of a wider city regional machinery grouped under the umbrella of the Manchester Growth Company, with an estimated £10 million invested in the wider city regional agenda.

This discussion of Manchester is not meant to devalue Liverpool's achievements. Manchester still faces almost as many challenges as Liverpool does on social issues. Rather it highlights some of the essential messages about building collaboration and trust at city region level around a compelling economic case. Those messages could be valuable to Liverpool in the coming years.

'Manchester does not have allies, it has interests. All partners pursue their own interest because they need each other. They don't necessarily love each other. But they respect each other and they know they need each other.' – Mike Emmerich, former chief executive, New Economy Manchester

This book has shown how arguments in the 1980s about the level of government funding to Liverpool led to a huge political crisis and threats of municipal bankruptcy, and ended in tears, with many Labour councillors disqualified from office and thrown out of the Labour Party. The consequences of that struggle blighted Liverpool's efforts to attract external investment for a very long time afterwards. In fact, as *Liverpool on the Brink* argued, the council had a good case that the level of cuts that the city had received was unfair. But the Labour council overplayed its hand. Joe Anderson was determined to avoid returning to those politics of protest and to try to manage his budget. But it can be argued that the impact of government cuts on the city's finances has been greater and more difficult to manage than those faced by the Militant Labour council in the 1980s. Local authority budgets are complex, contested and uncertain, and the national local government finance system constantly changes. But it is clear that Liverpool has experienced significant cuts in its resources that will make running the local authority and providing even its statutory services increasingly difficult in the immediate future.[5]

The impact of government cuts on Liverpool city region and city council

'The government purposefully gave us capital resources while cutting revenue. We had window boxes but the foundations were full of sewage.' – Ged Fitzgerald

Fiscal stress in Liverpool is the consequence of a national policy designed to impose austerity and reduce the size of the public sector and local government in particular. Many other cities have received large cuts in government support. The damage is not peculiar to Liverpool. Nevertheless, the scale of cuts has been greater in Liverpool than in the other large UK Core Cities. For example, in the first years of Coalition austerity between 2010 and 2014, the six Liverpool city region local authorities experienced £650 million in cuts. This was the equivalent of the first European Objective 1 programme. Liverpool local authority had the biggest cut of all the Core Cities. Within the city region, this cut was matched by Knowsley. So the two city region local authorities that were the highest ranked in the national Index of Multiple Deprivation received disproportionately heavy cuts to their funding from central government.[6]

The impact of government policy on Liverpool City Council has been as great as on the wider city region. The council is funded by a mix of government grants, council tax, which is determined locally, business rates, which are set nationally but with a proportion retained by local authorities, and some fees and charges. The balance between different sources of income has changed a lot in recent years. For example, from 2013/14 local authorities were allowed to keep up to 50% of business rates income, but the amount of general government grant was reduced. Effectively government grant, which was distributed on a relative needs basis, was largely replaced by business rates, which are inherently volatile and linked to local, national and international economic conditions, most of which are outside of the control of a local authority. This shifted the city council's ability to pay for services.

Cuts in national income

The changes in the local authority's financial position are best illustrated by the government's own formula known as Core Spending Power, which shows the money from government grants, the local share of business rates and council tax that the city council has to fund its services. From 2010/11 to 2019/20 Liverpool's spending power, based on the government's own figures, was reduced by £160 million. If it had received only the average level of cuts in spending power, it would have had a cut of £89 million and would have been £71 million better off in 2019/20. The total cut was equal to £712 per household, the eleventh highest in England. By comparison, the average cut across England was planned to be £320. In fact some authorities got an increase. Liverpool City Council calculated that it would have suffered a real-terms reduction in government funding of £444 million from 2010/11 to 2019/20 – the equivalent of a 64% cut.

A weak tax base

As central government funding has been reduced, local authorities have had to depend more on council tax and business rates. In 2010/11 council tax funded 13% of Liverpool's current expenditure. By 2016/17 local taxation, including business rates, funded 26%. Since funding from local taxation is more volatile than government grant funding, this makes it more difficult for local authorities to plan effectively and means that they are not only faced with shrinking resources but with increased uncertainty. Also the amount of income that can be raised from council tax depends heavily on the property tax base in the area. Liverpool has a low property tax base. In 2017 60% of its dwellings were in the lowest tax band A, over 77% in bands A and B, and 90% in the lowest three bands A–C. By contrast the average for England was 24% in band A, 44% in bands A and B and 66% in bands A–C. Liverpool was also hit by the number of residents

who qualified for discounts and exemptions. Its tax base in 2018/19 was reduced by almost 36% because of this, compared with the average reduction across England of 16%. Liverpool City Council raises an average of £866 in council tax for each dwelling and is ranked 313th lowest out of 326 English local authorities. The average amount raised per dwelling nationally is £1,185, with the highest, Surrey, raising £1,985, 2.3 times more than Liverpool. If Liverpool had the same proportion of dwellings in each tax band as nationally and the same proportion of discounts and exemptions, instead of £166.9 million in council tax income in 2018/19, it would have generated £264.6 million.

Limited business rates

Liverpool is also constrained by the nature of the business rate system, which is becoming an increasingly important part of its income. The amount that can be generated from business rates is based upon the number, size and types of businesses in an area and the extent to which they qualify for reliefs. For 2018/19 Liverpool City Council forecast that its business rates yield would be £187 million. The average for the eight Core Cities was £248 million, with Liverpool the sixth lowest. As important is the amount that it generates per head of population. In 2018/19 Liverpool City Council could raise £393 per head. Across England the average was £452 per head. Again, Liverpool was sixth lowest out of the Core Cities. Manchester generated £613 per head. Eleven authorities, mostly in London or the South-East, were forecasting business rates income in 2018/19 above £1,000 per head. The highest, Westminster, generated £8,954, followed by Camden with £2,663 per head.

Frontline cuts

How did this affect Liverpool's spending on services after 2010 when the city mayor was elected? In fact, the amount spent on frontline services – education, housing, planning and development, environmental and regulatory services, cultural services, highways and transport services – was reduced significantly. The exceptions were children and adult social care. For example, spending on education services was reduced from £469 million to £383 million, a cut of 18%. In 2010/11 education made up 38% of the council's current expenditure. In 2016/17 this had been reduced to 33%. The city council's current expenditure fell by £148.8 million or 12%. The equivalent cut across England was 10%. Despite these pressures, the city council continued to set long-term balanced budgets. For the three years 2014–17 it made a cut of 25% in statutory services and 50% in non-statutory services such as youth provision. It took 50% out of direct service provision, which meant that staff numbers were cut by half. Cuts to the voluntary sector were 25%. Given Liverpool's travails with government in the 1980s, there were always suspicions that the council was shroud waving and exaggerating the scale of the impact upon the city. Equally there were concerns that the Labour mayor might go down the path of confrontation. But neither was true. The mayor was determined not to act illegally. He used up council reserves, which fell from £248 million in 2010 to £37 million in 2017. He cut 3,000 staff. In 2017 he argued that if he closed all libraries, sports centres and parks and stopped streetlights, road maintenance and street cleaning, he would only save £68 million rather than the £90 million he was expected to save. So he cut adult social care by a further 10%.

Nor was the city council exaggerating. The council's auditor, Grant Thornton, reported that it was possible in 2017/18 that the local authority would no longer be able to deliver discretionary services and that in 2018/19 the council could reach a tipping point where it could no longer pay for mandatory services. This was despite the fact that, in their view as auditors, the council had good financial planning and a track record of delivering savings. Their judgement was that the council and the mayor were actively managing the challenge of continuing to deliver public services in the face of significant budget pressures.[7] Of course, such financial pressures were not peculiar to Liverpool. But the cuts were more severe than in many other places and they were made just as its economy was also being hit by a downturn in the national economy.

Government welfare changes make it worse

The cuts to Liverpool City Council's budget were aggravated by the financial impact of the welfare reforms that were being introduced by the government. A Joseph Rowntree Foundation study, for example, showed how hard Liverpool's residents would be hit by the changes.[8] The loss between 2010 and 2016 was £157 million and was predicted to be a further £145 million between 2016 and 2021. Liverpool, which was the fourth most deprived local authority in the country, had had the fifth highest loss from welfare reform by 2016 and would be sixth hardest hit by 2021. The loss for each working-age adult by 2016 was £480 - the 29th largest cut for all local authorities. It was predicted by 2021 to be £900 – the 31st largest cut. The cuts would be greatest for families with dependent children, including lone parents and social housing tenants. Social housing tenants would receive a cut of £1,690 by 2021 in comparison with £730 for those in the private rental sector and £290 in owner-occupied housing. The city council calculated that the combined loss of £292 million by 2021 was likely to lead to a loss of 2,000 jobs because of reduced consumer spending. It was predicting significant increases in child poverty and income inequality by 2021. And the greatest hits would be felt by the poorest people living in the already most-deprived areas of the city, especially, although not exclusively, in north Liverpool, and in the south of the city in Belle Vale, Speke Garston and the inner wards surrounding the city centre. These cuts to the city council's revenue budget and its residents' welfare income only underlined the shift in the city's financial position in recent years as private-sector investment in capital projects, especially in the city centre, continued to grow as the city council's ability to provide basic statutory services was falling. Liverpool was becoming capital rich and revenue poor. As one current councillor put it, 'We thought the system would crash. To keep it going we borrowed and had to certify

it was prudential. But we can't do that in future. We have maxed out the city credit cards on totemic projects. It is not sustainable in the long term. We are now on the road to hit a massive brick wall.' This has important and different implications for the richer and poorer people and communities across the city.

The balance sheet on progress in the age of austerity

In 2019 Liverpool, Janus-like as ever, presented two faces to the external world – economically, socially, culturally and politically. There were still big challenges in all of these areas. But the overriding sense was one of progress with flaws, rather than of failure to progress. Leadership, governance and politics seemed more robust even though city regional issues and tensions remained. The city had avoided returning to the politics of confrontation, despite the huge fiscal pressures on the council. Development was continuing apace across the city centre, despite some concerns about the nature and quality of some of the projects, as well as some well-rehearsed problems with a limited number of development schemes that had collapsed financially. The economic picture was more robust even though social challenges were still large, and there were fears that worse were to come as austerity hit harder. The final chapter attempts to draw up a balance sheet on past performance and future prospects. Before that, the next chapter digs deeper into the fundamentals of Liverpool's economy to see the extent to which it will in future be able to sustain the remaking of a post-imperial city.

Notes

1 Michael Parkinson, *Liverpool's Elected Mayor 2012-16: An Independent Assessment* (Heseltine Institute, University of Liverpool, 2016).

2 Parkinson et al., *Second Tier Cities*; Michael Parkinson, 'UK City Regions: Policies, Performance and Prospects', *Town Planning Review*, 87.6 (2016); Parkinson and Meegan, 'Economic Place Making'; Philip McCann, *The UK Regional-National Economic Problem* (Routledge, 2016).

3 Michael Parkinson, Richard Meegan, Jay Karecha and Richard Evans, *The State of Liverpool City Region Report* (Heseltine Institute, University of Liverpool, 2016).

4 Michael Parkinson, *Policy Messages for Liverpool City Region and the LEP*, report to the NWDA, and Liverpool City Council (2010); Parkinson et al., *State of Liverpool City Region Report*.

5 Tony Wells, 'The State of Liverpool City Finances', personal note to the author (Liverpool City Council, 2018); *Cities Outlook 2019* (Centre for Cities, 2019).

6 Parkinson et al., *State of Liverpool City Region Report*.

7 Grant Thornton, *The Guardian*, 10 November 2015.

8 Christina Beatty and Steve Fothergill, *The Uneven Impact of Welfare Reform* (Joseph Rowntree Foundation, 2016).

CHAPTER SIX

The state of Liverpool's economy today

This book has looked at the renaissance of Liverpool during the past thirty years as its leaders responded to its demise as a globally connected imperial city. It has shown how they tried to deal with the impact of post-imperial economic decline on its political, physical, social and financial infrastructure and behaviour. It has assessed the impact of a range of initiatives designed to regenerate Liverpool city centre and to underpin it with a more sustainable economy. It has shown how those initiatives, which were often externally generated by European or national government, gradually combined to regenerate and reconnect parts of the city into a more coherent place. Liverpool is going through a successful if still incomplete process of renaissance that has better equipped it to survive in a globally challenging economy. But this book has also shown that not all places or people have shared in the fruits of the city's success.

This book has focused on the physical renewal of the city because this has been the primary focus of Liverpool's leaders since the collapse of the Militant Tendency regime in the late 1980s. The scale of the renewal challenge meant that this was inevitable. Many regeneration initiatives were impressive, well regarded and often nationally significant. The approach worked. Nevertheless, this approach will not be enough to ensure that in future Liverpool is a serious economic player at a European let alone global level. That will need a clearer focus on economic competitiveness beyond the regeneration of particular parts of the city, however important they are currently. The city will have to develop its assets and the drivers of a modern successful city region. It will also need a change of scale. Until relatively recently the effort to regenerate Liverpool has focused mainly though not exclusively on the city, in particular its centre. But economic logic as well as national policy means that Liverpool cannot

Antony Gormley,
Another Place,
Crosby beach
© eye35/Alamy Stock
Photo

operate at that scale in future. Its challenges will have to be met at the level of the city region – economically, socially, environmentally and politically. Given these economic realities, this chapter moves beyond the story of the historic renaissance of the city of Liverpool to examine the fundamental position of the Liverpool city region economy. It looks at some of the hard evidence about – but also some perceptions of – its performance and prospects. It draws heavily on the *State of the Liverpool City Region Report*, which collected a huge amount of hard, quantitative data about the city region's economy as well as the views of many of its senior players regarding its performance and prospects. These issues were also raised by Michael Heseltine and Terry Leahy's influential report in 2011, *Rebalancing Britain*, the Foresight work for the Department for Business, Innovation and Skills (BIS), led by Professor Alan Harding in 2015, the economic analysis led by Professor Alex Lord from the Heseltine Institute in 2017 and the Liverpool city region LEP's Growth Strategy 2016.[1]

How did Liverpool city region's economy perform in the boom and bust?

The prospects of success for Liverpool city region will at least in part depend on the capacity, willingness and commitment of its leadership class. Here, there is cause for optimism. The mood music among those players across Liverpool is far better than it has been in recent decades. There is a remarkable degree of agreement on the big issues: how much Liverpool has improved in the past fifteen years; what its outstanding challenges are; who needs to do what better or differently in future. There is considerable optimism within the city region about its future, despite wider national and global economic uncertainty. The views of many people from outside the city are actually more positive than those of some within. In particular, the view from government, in significant contrast perhaps to its recent view of Liverpool, is positive rather than negative. Ministers want and need Liverpool city region to perform well in future if government is to deliver its devolution agenda.

Liverpool city region in the boom
So the political mood music around the place is as good as it has been in many years. But is this optimism borne out by reality? This is some evidence that it is. During the boom Liverpool made real improvements in jobs, productivity and population. It made some improvements on the key drivers of performance – skills, diversity, connectivity, innovation and place quality. It achieved a substantial amount of successful physical regeneration, especially around Liverpool city centre. The economic baseline is now higher and the trend positive. A Liverpool LEP report in 2018 provided a positive snapshot of the achievements of Liverpool city region during the previous decade.[2] Between 2008 and 2018 the city region had over 100 major investments totalling over £10 billion which helped create

24,000 additional jobs and 8,000 additional businesses. It had a wealth of globally competitive and innovative sectors, including health and life sciences, digital and creative, advanced manufacturing and renewable energy. Through its ports and airport, it was a global gateway for trade and investment for the Northern Powerhouse and the wider UK. It was home to some of the world's leading international businesses and a range of globally competitive exporters. It hosted world-class assets such as the Liverpool School of Tropical Medicine, Liverpool2, Sensor City and the Materials Innovation Factory. It had globally significant research and development in infectious diseases, high-performance computing and materials chemistry. It was increasingly attracting international investment in its major development and infrastructure projects including offshore wind farms.

The digital creative and enhanced intelligence sectors had expanded, with 3,500 businesses such as IBM Research, Unilever, SciTech Daresbury and Telefonica/O2 employing 11,000 people and contributing £1.3 billion. It had three transatlantic fibre optic cable connections, was a testbed for 5G and had growth three times faster than the England average in the previous decade. Advanced manufacturing had 3,000 companies, including leading international companies such as Jaguar Land Rover, Unilever, Pilkington, Ineos and Astra Zeneca, Getrag Ford, Alstom, Cammell Laird, Johnson's Controls and ABB, which employed 47,000 people and contributed £3.3 billion to the economy. Its productivity was 7.7% above the UK average. Health and life sciences were major strengths with Ely Lilly, Sequirus, Astra Zeneca, Bristol Myers Squib and Mast group, four universities and a series of major hospitals employing 125,000 people, 20% of the city region's workforce, and contributing £4.4 billion to the city region's economy. The port and logistics sector had major companies such as Peel Ports, Bibby Group, AVL, Maersk Transglobal Express, QVC and Stobart Group, which employed 20,000 people, contributing £1 billion to the economy. Peel Ports had invested over £1 billion in the port, which remains the closest port to over 50% of UK manufacturing and the largest Atlantic-facing port. Liverpool2 deep water can take vessels coming through the Panama Canal and up to 95% of the world's vessels. The low-carbon energy sector with world-class companies such as Orsted, ABB, Cadent, Drax, Innogy and Clarke Energy was growing, having invested £4.3 billion in offshore wind farms, employing 35,000 people in 1,500 firms and contributing £2 billion to the economy. The tourist economy – which twenty years earlier was not regarded as a serious contributor – had been immensely successful and had expanded during the past decade, so that Liverpool, with its huge range of cultural and sporting assets, became the fifth most internationally visited city in the UK. The sector employed 54,000 people with 10,000 added in the previous ten years, attracted 60 million visitors and contributed £4.3 billion to the city region's GVA. One of the largest contributors to the city regional economy was business and professional services, with a range of banks, insurance companies, consultancy companies, financial advisers and

law firms supporting 107,000 jobs in 10,000 businesses and contributing £8.4 billion to the city regional economy.

However, despite these real strengths and despite its good boom, Liverpool city region still compares unfavourably with the other four big city regions in the Northern Powerhouse – Manchester, Sheffield, Leeds and Newcastle – as the LEP report demonstrated. In urban economies, scale matters. Despite its recent recovery after decades of decline, the Liverpool economy is still too small. For example, its population at 1.53 million is smaller than those of the other four, with Manchester and Leeds, the regional capitals of the north, twice as big. The size of its total economy at £30 million is smaller than the others, with again Greater Manchester and Leeds over twice as big. Its GVA per head at £20,125 is again smaller than its northern competitors. The better news is that in terms of GVA per hours worked, at £30 Liverpool is better than every other city region and the northern average of £29. The explanation is that its workers are productive, but there are too few jobs and therefore too few people working in them. This is reflected in its employment rate, which is the lowest of the big city regions across the Northern Powerhouse at 55%. Its problem of youth unemployment is even worse. It has the lowest employment rate for 16–24 year olds at 48% in contrast with the northern average of 53%.

The position on skills is equally challenging. It has the second-highest level of people with no qualifications at 11%, the highest level of people with a maximum skill level of NVQ2 at 20%, the third-lowest percentage of people with NVQ4 at 31%, and the second-lowest percentage of people with a trade apprenticeship at 3%. Perhaps most importantly, it has too few firms. Liverpool's business density rate, the number of firms per 10,000 of the adult population, in 2018 was 366.2, in comparison with Leeds at 468.2 and Manchester at 506.8. It needs 17,000 more firms to reach the national average. As the LEP report underlined, Liverpool city region needs more jobs, more skills, more apprenticeships, more businesses, more high-growth businesses – and accelerated growth.

That is the structure. But what about the trend and performance of the city region economy? In fact it had a very good boom. After decades of decline it increased its jobs, output and population. For example, between 1984 and 1996 employment in the city region fell by 12%. But recovery started in 1997 and in the next six years employment grew faster than the national rate. Up to the recession in 2008, employment increased by 15%. And even after years of recession and austerity, employment in the city region in 2014 was still almost 19% higher than it had been in 1996. But the recession and austerity years did slow employment growth. After 2009 employment in the city region grew at just above a quarter of the national rate and below London and many other city regions. But there was a decent improvement in output and productivity. GVA in the Liverpool city region economy grew on average by 2.9% annually over the boom decade. This was, however, below the national growth rate of 3.7% overall. Just as employment and output picked up, so too did population. After years of continuous and severe decline through the 1980s and 1990s, there was an upturn after the early 2000s and notably since the 2008 recession. Population had increased by just over 31,000 since 2001, an increase of 2.1%, although this is significantly lower than the rate for England as a whole, 9.3%, and that of other city regions. So Liverpool city region still faces many challenges. There is a wealth gap. There is a jobs gap, with low employment and high unemployment levels, especially for young people. There is a skills gap. There is a productivity gap. There is an income gap with relatively low household incomes, partly reflecting economic inactivity and the greater dependence on benefits and state pensions. There is a poverty gap – the city region still contains some of the country's most economically and socially disadvantaged neighbourhoods.

Liverpool city's economy in austerity – some good but some bad news
Since the city of Liverpool has been the focus of this book, it is worth seeing how the city itself performed during austerity in comparison with the wider city region, but also with the other UK Core Cities and the UK as a whole. In fact the picture is mixed, with both good and bad news.[3] In some ways Liverpool performed better than other UK cities. Between 2010 and 2016 the number of employees in the city increased by 4% more than the city region, the other Core Cities and the nation. It gained 17,000 jobs in this period, an increase of 7%. This is higher than the city region but still below the Core Cities and the national average. The mix of private- and public-sector jobs also shifted during austerity, although not as much as in the other Core Cities or the nation. Importantly

the city increased the number of private-sector jobs by 15% – more than the city region but just less than the Core Cities and the nation. Public-sector jobs declined by 10%, but still less than the city region, the Core Cities and national rates of 13%. In 2016 25% of its jobs were in the public sector – again several points higher than the others. Also many of the jobs created in the period 2010–16 were part time. In 2016 36% of its jobs were part time, just above the city region, Core Cities and national rates. 12,000 of them were created after 2010, an increase of 16%, twice the national average. Its increase in full-time jobs was less than half the Core Cities and national average. In 2017 average full-time pay for a Liverpool resident was £25,863, lower than the Core Cities and considerably lower than the national average of £28,833. Earnings increased by 8% from 2010 but below the national rate.

The position of Liverpool's businesses during the recession similarly showed some good and less good news. In 2017 there were over 17,000 businesses in Liverpool, a third of the total in the city region. In that year the number of businesses actually grew by over 7.2% – faster than the city region, the Core Cities and the national average. Between 2010 and 2017 the number grew by over 3,000 at 26.6% – higher than the city region and national average but lower than the Core Cities. However, there are fewer businesses in Liverpool than in other places. Liverpool's business density rate is 70% of the national average. But the city did improve its performance between 2006 and 2016 by 35.2% – higher than the city regional and the national rates although lower than the Core Cities. Liverpool started 2,670 businesses in 2016, more than in

St Paul's Square, interior
© McCoy Wynne
(mccoywynne.co.uk)

any year since 2005. The city's survival rate of recently formed firms was 52% – lower than the others.

The Liverpool economy did well in the boom, but less well in austerity. During 1998–2016 the total GVA of Liverpool grew by 99%, faster than all the others. But the trend was reversed during austerity, when its growth increased at 5%, in comparison with the city region at 11%, the Core Cities at 20% and the UK rate of 24%. The same trend was true for GVA per resident. During the boom years it had been closing the gap with other places. In the period 1998–2016 Liverpool's GVA per head increased by 86%, higher than the rest. But during austerity its growth was lower at only 0.8% in comparison with the city region at 9%, the Core Cities at 12% and the nation at 18%. In 1998 it was 83% of the national rate. By 2010 it had improved so that it was at 104% of the national level. But by 2016 it had dropped back to 88%, with the Core Cities at 105%. As we saw earlier, Liverpool's problem is not productivity per worker but per resident. In other words, the workers are productive but not enough people actually work. There is a shortage of jobs. So, for example, productivity per worker in 2016 was 86.9% of the national rate. By contrast the Core Cities figure, which was much higher for residents, was slightly lower than Liverpool for workers. But between 2010 and 2016 productivity in Liverpool fell by 8% in contrast to the Core Cities fall of only 2%. Connected to this, gross disposable family income per head in Liverpool is relatively low. In 2015 it was £14,833, £727 below the Core Cities average and £4,273 lower than the national average. So as with the city region overall, Liverpool's baseline is higher now than in the past. It made a lot of progress in the boom, closing the gap with some other cities. But austerity has pulled it – and many of its residents – back. The challenges remain.

The drivers of competitiveness

It is clear from the evidence above that Liverpool and Liverpool city region, despite some progress, lag behind some other city regions in important ways. The question is why? What explains its uneven performance? To establish this requires some agreement regarding what a successful urban economy is. At its most simple it is a place where people want – and have an opportunity – to work, invest, live, study and play. My work in the UK and Europe suggests that successful cities have more rather than less of the following: economic diversity; skilled human capital; innovation; connectivity; place quality; and the strategic leadership capacity to deliver sustainable development. I discuss these drivers of economic competitiveness next. I then look at where Liverpool stands on these drivers in comparison with ten UK city regions, including London.

Economic diversity
The cities that are most successful in responding to economic change are least dependent on a single sector. Those that depend entirely upon a single sector

– whether old-fashioned coal, steel or shipping, or new-fashioned financial services, mobile telephones, culture or computers – are most vulnerable to the vagaries of global economic forces. Economic diversity matters. A successful city will have strength in global and local firms, large and small, manufacturing as well as services, the old as well as the new economy. It will constantly seek to diversify its economic base, pushing into different sectors – but not indiscriminately. Cities need to diversify and to deepen existing strengths. They cannot build on strengths where none currently exist. The trick is to work with what they have and to modernise. There is a continuing debate about the merits of old versus new economies. The lesson from Europe is that both matter.

Human capital and skills

A skilled workforce is a critical feature of city productivity. Modern economies increasingly depend upon knowledge-intensive sectors, even within manufacturing. Policy makers and businesses typically rate this as the most significant single success factor. Increasingly, cities need people who have the skills that businesses want. This involves vocational as well as traditional academic education, so colleges as well as universities matter. However, a crucial factor is not simply the presence of a skilled workforce but the relationship between the suppliers and consumers of that labour in the universities, colleges, research institutes, government and private sectors – the so-called triple helix.

Graduating students in Philharmonic Hall
Image courtesy of the University of Liverpool

Innovation

Innovation – the introduction of new or changed processes, services or forms of organisation into the market place – is perhaps the most crucial characteristic of a successful city region. The OECD estimates that in the past thirty years more than half the total growth in output of the developed world resulted from innovation. Four features lead to urban competitiveness: investment in modern, knowledge-based physical equipment; investment in research and education; investment in innovation; and labour productivity. In all of these, knowledge and innovation are closely linked, the main drivers of place competitiveness. Successful city regions make innovation not a single idea or a product, but a key feature of the way they organise their affairs and do their business.

Connectivity

Connectivity is also crucial. It is partly physical – trains, planes, motorways, ICT. It is partly cultural – having international horizons and connections. The most successful city regions have the physical and electronic infrastructure to move goods, services and people quickly and efficiently within and between cities. External connections are important, since exporting remains critical to success. So airports, ports, road and rail infrastructure are critical. They encourage face-to-face communication, which has been supplemented but not replaced by technological communication. However, connectivity is not simply physical. It has a cultural dimension. Successful cities have clear internationalisation strategies and invest in international networking to raise their profile, gain new allies, expand market share, influence decision makers and learn new strategies and practices.

Place quality

People typically move to cities to get jobs – preferably good ones. But often they stay because of the quality of life there.[4] Smart decision makers understand the significance of attracting and retaining skilled workers to their cities. And they recognise that the quality of life for workers and their families is an increasingly important factor. So places with the assets of a good environment, distinctive architecture, cultural facilities, quality housing stock and access to natural amenities attempt to preserve and improve them. This can help drive up land values, which in turn makes private-sector investment and development more likely. This improves the scale and quality of cities' physical offer – office, retail, leisure, residential – which in turn encourages economic growth. But place quality is not simply about the physical or natural environment or culture. Its wider social dimension – social cohesion and social capital – is also critical. So the quality of public services in a city – education, health, housing, transport, culture and welfare – is a crucial dimension of place quality and hence success. City leaders need the resources and policy levers to be able to invest in and improve those crucial services if their cities are to succeed.

Leadership and governance

City leaders' room for manoeuvre is affected by wider forces such as globalisation, long-term economic changes and national policies and performance. Cities cannot simply reinvent themselves. They must start from where they are in terms of economic and social structures. Nevertheless, economic competitiveness strategies do not just emerge – they can and must be fashioned and implemented. And they take a long time to develop and put into practice. Leadership in its widest sense is crucial to this process. Successful cities have the leadership to exploit their assets to develop new economic futures for themselves, their businesses and residents. The experience of leading European cities underlines the importance of leaders in shaping strategies or influencing key programmes; partnerships between key players in the public and private sectors; and having allies to influence the decisions of national governments. So, successful cities have effective political and administrative leaders, long-term commitment to strategic agendas, the ability to reconcile shifting agendas, the willingness to take calculated risks and the capacity to actively involve public- and private-sector partners. Although they are clichés, the experience of successful city regions emphasises the importance of vision, leadership, partnership and mature politics.

Where does Liverpool city region stand on the drivers of competitiveness?

Is it sufficiently economically diverse?

In fact the economy is reasonably diverse. The SOLCRR showed that it is less diversified than the two other Northern Powerhouse city regions, Manchester and Leeds, as well as Birmingham and Bristol. But it is less specialised than London and several other large city regions. It has sometimes been argued that the Liverpool city region economy is too public-sector dominated. In part that is an oversimplification. The kind of public-sector jobs – for example high or low value added – is important. That said, the balance has been changing in the recent austerity years: 20,400 jobs were lost in the public sector in the city region and 25,900 gained in the private sector, a net gain of 5,500 jobs. Liverpool city region had the third-highest loss of public-sector jobs after Bristol and Newcastle-upon Tyne – nearly 16%, one and a half times the national fall. By contrast, private-sector jobs grew by 7% – below the national rate but above that of five other city regions. The result of these changes is that the public sector now accounts for just over 21% of Liverpool's total workforce. This is less than that of Cardiff, Glasgow, Edinburgh and Newcastle.

A diverse economy should also be able to create new firms. How does Liverpool perform? The city region ranked fifth in terms of the average number of active enterprises operating in the recession and austerity years. During this period, its net birth and death rate of enterprises was above five of the other city regions. But it was still below the national rate and only around a quarter of the rates in London and Edinburgh. And it had the lowest survival rate for enterprises set up in the recession year, 2008, of all city regions. This performance was qualified, however, by the positive net birth and death rate in 2013. The city region had the highest rate of all the city regions and one and half times the national rate, suggesting a degree of post-recession resilience. The rate of self-employment is another measure of enterprise activity, often being the first step into entrepreneurial behaviour for many people. The rate in Liverpool city region has improved over recent years. The proportion who are self-employed has increased from 8.6% in 2004 to 11% in 2014. But it still lags behind the UK average of 13.9%.

Are its skills good enough?

Despite significant knowledge assets, the city region is still low on science, research, engineering and technology occupations and high-level qualifications, and high on no qualifications. In part this is the historical legacy of its industrial past, which did not encourage the development of high-level, technical skills. So the city region faces a real challenge in its skills base, and especially, if its ambitions are to be met, in developing and retaining skills in the knowledge economy. It is well below the national average on residents employed in science, research, engineering and technology professions, ranked ninth of the ten city regions in the SOLCRR. It performs relatively well in retaining the students who graduate from its universities. Nearly 48% of students who studied in the city region found employment in it, the fourth-highest of the ten second-tier city regions. There are still not enough graduate jobs to retain all the students who study in the city region. Liverpool city region needs to create more graduate-level jobs to absorb those whom it educates and also to attract graduates from outside. Despite recent improvements, the city region has a long-standing deficit of people with higher-level qualifications and an above-average proportion of people with no qualifications. It remains the second-worst performer in terms of the former and the third-worst in terms of the latter.

Is Liverpool innovative enough?

Liverpool faces many different challenges on this driver. For example, in terms of business enterprise expenditure on R&D, Liverpool ranked eighth of the ten city regions studied in the SOLCRR, though it is higher than many other city regions. But there is some better news. The share of employment in science and technology businesses is one indication of innovation capacity. Overall, the city region has roughly the national share of these sectors and sits in the middle of the city region rankings. It has greater than national shares for two of the sectors: life sciences and healthcare and other scientific/technological manufacture. But Liverpool lags behind on the number of people employed in small- and medium-sized enterprises, which are knowledge-intensive business services. It also lags in terms of employees in SME firms in the creative industries.

Is Liverpool well enough connected?

In fact, Liverpool's connectivity has been greatly enhanced by the recent expansion of the airport. In 2014 it handled nearly six times the number of passengers that it did seventeen years earlier – a growth rate that massively outstripped national growth. Growth has been hit by the recession, however, and passenger numbers have still to recover to their pre-recession peak. The port remains a vital part of the city region's economy, central to the logistics industry and the Atlantic Gateway project. There has been a dramatic recovery in port traffic since 1987, after an equally dramatic fall from the mid-1960s. As nationally, growth has been hit by the 2008 recession and, after a brief recovery in 2011–12, traffic is still below the 2005 peak. The picture on broadband connectivity is mixed. The city region ranks fourth of second-tier city regions in superfast broadband availability and average download speed, but falls to sixth in take-up of lines. For all its connections, the city region still has the lowest proportion of its employment in export-intensive industries of all the second-tier city regions. And not being directly connected to HS2 would present another challenge for Liverpool.

Is its place quality good enough?

Liverpool has a wealth of architectural and cultural assets and heritage. It has more Grade 1 listed buildings than any city outside London. It is the only city region with a UNESCO-recognised World Heritage Site, the waterfront. In National Museums Liverpool, it has the only national museum service in England outside London. And it has a host of art galleries – notably Tate Liverpool – sporting and music venues, events and festivals. The strength of the city region's cultural attractions is reflected in the fact that it attracts an estimated 60 million visitors a year, as well as by Liverpool's current status as the fifth most-visited city in the UK. It has become an increasingly self-confident city, with a flourishing city centre scene that attracts its own residents, 54,000 students as well as short- and long-term visitors. The quality of the cultural, retail, leisure, music, sporting and food offer is much higher than it was a decade ago – and certainly miles better than in the heyday of the Beatles! If you have a good job it is a very good place to live. So in many ways for many people the quality of place in Liverpool is attractive.

However, as we saw earlier, those assets and attractions have to be set alongside the social and economic challenges that the city faces. Incomes, skills and educational attainment levels are lower than in many other cities, and rates of unemployment, especially of young people, morbidity and mortality, worklessness and dependency on state benefits are higher. Liverpool also faces significant housing challenges. There have been improvements, including the scale of new-build, attempts to address housing decline in the inner core, investment in social housing with stock transfer, and the creation of a market for city centre living. But the quality, age, location and type are limited. 68% of properties across the city region are currently in the low council tax bands A and B, and only 16% in band D or above. There are 16,400 long-term empty

homes. Its low average incomes are reflected in low house prices. In the SOLCRR only Newcastle-upon-Tyne and Sheffield had lower median house prices than Liverpool. Liverpool's housing offer needs to be improved in terms of variety, quality and affordability. So despite cultural, environmental and historical assets and despite the many improvements across the city, Liverpool faces constraints in terms of the quality and range of its public services and the economic and social conditions of many of its people and communities. Austerity will not help this.

Is its leadership and strategic decision-making capacity good enough?

On five drivers of performance – skills, diversity, connectivity, innovation and place quality – Liverpool city region has made progress. But there is further to go. How well does it perform on the final driver – decision-making capacity? The headline message is that it is getting much better. Many believe that the elected city mayor has been a success and has improved governance capacity in Liverpool. Relations between the different parts of the city region have also been improving. Relations between the public and private sectors, if not perfect, are certainly much improved from earlier decades. The mood music across the city is far better than in earlier times, with key decision makers more optimistic about the future of the place. There is also greater awareness of the city's achievements and remaining challenges. There is great realism among key players about how far the city has come, yet how far it has still to go. In both cases this is a long way. In particular Liverpool has two elected mayors, because the city cooperated with government in 2012 and introduced an elected city mayor several years before government policy required city regional mayors to be elected. Whether that dual system will be the right one for the next decade remains to be determined.

There is widespread agreement within and beyond the city region across all the different sectors about how far Liverpool has come in recent years and how far it still has to go. There is agreement that the city has undergone a dramatic transformation. The city centre, the waterfront and Liverpool One are commonly acknowledged as major transformations. The success of the port and the contribution of the universities, the hospitals and the visitor economy are well recognised. But everyone recognises that other places have similarly improved, so the gap is not necessarily closing. Everyone is agreed that productivity levels are too low. Skill levels are too low. Employment is too low and unemployment too high. Rental levels are too low. The housing market is too homogeneous. Office quality and transport connections need to be improved. Too many parts of the city region have not shared in the prosperity. There is a real concern that the achievements of the renaissance have not been translated into the lives of too many ordinary people, some of whom live very close to the regenerated city centre. More specifically there are worries about whether the next generation of young people can see and will get an opportunity to be successful in Liverpool's future. To tackle these challenges Liverpool leaders will need to help create, attract and retain better jobs; raise skill levels and retain skilled people; increase connectivity; encourage more innovation; improve place quality and in particular address the problems of the people and places excluded from the economic successes it has had.

'The statistics hide the gap within the city region. You can obviously see the developments in Liverpool in the city centre and waterfront. But across the region loads of people have been left behind. We are plugging away getting our patch up the league tables. The relativities may have changed. But the same people and places are stuck in the same place.' – Business association leader

While there is a degree of realism about the economic, social and environmental challenges that the city region still faces, the mood is wildly different from a decade ago. Liverpool city region has had success. It does function relatively well as an integrated labour market. It has a range of complementary economic strengths. It had some real success in the boom years. It has achieved a substantial amount of successful physical regeneration, especially around Liverpool city centre. The city's baseline is higher and the trend is positive. But it started from a low base, and it lags on many of the key drivers of economic competitiveness. The position is challenging but not impossible. And Liverpool is not uniquely challenged by these issues. Many other UK city regions have similar problems and challenges. Liverpool has no cause for unrealistic optimism – but nor for undue pessimism.

Notes

1   Michael Heseltine and Terry Leahy,
    Rebalancing Britain: Policy or Slogan?
    Liverpool City Region Building on its
    Strengths (2011); Alan Harding et
    al., *Liverpool City Region Foresight*
    Prospectus, report to BIS (2015); Alex
    Lord et al., *An Agenda for Liverpool*
    City Region (Heseltine Institute,
    University of Liverpool, 2017); LCR
    LEP, *Building Our Future: Liverpool*
    City Region Growth Strategy (2016).

2   Mark Basnett, *Liverpool City Region*
    Today: Challenges and Opportunities
    and the Role of the LEP (LCR Local
    Enterprise Partnership, 2018).

3   Liverpool City Council, *Liverpool*
    Economic Briefing – A Monitor of Jobs,
    Business and Economic Growth (2018).

4   Sako Musterd and Alan Murie,
    Making Competitive Cities (Wiley,
    2012).

CHAPTER SEVEN

Liverpool beyond the brink: what are the lessons and what is to be done?

This book has tried to show how and why Liverpool has taken the path it has during the past thirty years. It has argued that the city has gone from being a bad news story on the newspapers' front pages for all the wrong reasons to a good news story in the public eye for the right reasons. Given where the city was in the 1980s, it is extraordinary how far it has come and how much it has changed. The city, its leaders and people are more confident, more optimistic, more ambitious and more positive. The city has improved its performance on some of the economic fundamentals. It has seriously exploited its cultural and heritage assets to present a very different picture to the world, nationally and internationally. People are voting with their feet. After a dramatic decline, the city's population is growing again – up 50,000 in this century, faster than the nation in recent years and predicted to be half a million by 2020. It is also becoming younger and more ethnically diverse – a real break with the recent past. The mood music is far better than at any time since the 1960s and Beatlemania. Political relations have improved, particularly during the past decade. The different parts of the city have been gradually put together again physically. The post-imperial city is being remade.

'We have turned the liner.' – Max Steinberg, former chief executive, Liverpool Vision

But it's still not perfect. Too many places and people have not shared in the city's renaissance. The social challenges are still big. Political relationships are much better but still need strengthening. The city's capacity to deliver regeneration is impressive, but its capacity to deliver economic competitiveness needs to be

Old and new: Royal Liver building alongside modern glass buildings
© Sally Anderson/ Alamy Stock Photo

increased. And despite improvements, the city needs to do better on some of the key drivers of success. This final chapter pulls these threads together and does three things. First, it identifies some of the lessons for Liverpool, national government and a wider international audience about the city's renaissance. Second, it reflects on the contribution of the key players who raised the aspirations and ambition of the city. Finally, it identifies three key strategic challenges for the city as it tries to build on the progress it has made in the past two decades: productivity, people and place.

What were the lessons of success?

The public sector was crucial
The proper role of the state and the market in cities remains contested territory. Arguments about the right balance between public and private intervention have ebbed and flowed dramatically during the past thirty years. For many of those years it was assumed that the public sector was the problem and the private the solution. Then public–private partnerships became the preferred model or relationship. More recently the travails of many of these models have led to a revision of the right relationship and to a reassessment of the importance of the public sector in city development. But whatever the debate about principles, it is clear that the public sector, for good or ill, has always been a decisive factor in Liverpool's performance and prospects. For example, the withdrawal of public money in the late 1970s and 1980s precipitated the political and fiscal crisis that damaged the city's reputation, self-image, self-confidence and economic performance for two decades. It deterred even the modest investment that might have come to the city. Equally the poor quality of local government public services at that time contributed to the relative unattractiveness of the city for external investors.

But this book has also underlined more positively that many of the critical stages of the city's comeback were underpinned by public-sector intervention, which took the initial risk out of development and encouraged subsequent private-sector investment. The Merseyside Task Force, the Merseyside Development Corporation, the European Commission Objective 1 programme, City Challenge, Speke Garston Development Company and Partnership, the European Capital of Culture, City Focus, the North West Regional Development Agency, Liverpool Vision and Knowledge Quarter Liverpool were all either publicly initiated or funded in one form or another. They were all crucial to the city's renaissance. Nobody can know what Liverpool's trajectory would have been without this range of public-sector interventions over three decades. But arguably its renaissance would have been delayed – or indeed may never have happened. In different ways the initiatives created ambition, hope and confidence for key partners. Liverpool is a clear example of the decisive role that the public sector can play in incentivising, rewarding or de-risking market-sector involvement. It underlines the wider policy point that in places where the private sector is weak or risk-averse, the public sector can play a crucial part in helping to create markets and make cities investable. The evidence of urban success in Europe only underlines this point.

It's not a quick fix

'It takes thirty years to become an overnight success.' – Tom Bloxham, Urban Splash

Another message from Liverpool's renaissance is that it took a long time. It is not yet by any means complete. It has been built on the efforts of many different players at different times in the past thirty years. The foundations for success in one era were often laid by different people in previous eras. It was slow, grinding work. Certainly, the city's renaissance could not be taken for granted, and often it seemed that it might not pay off. The people who started the waterfront development in the 1980s would be pleased but possibly surprised to see how successful the process they started has become. Local and national leaders need to stick at it.

External intervention and a culture of confidence, ambition, aspiration

A third message is that the stimulus for change – at least at the beginning of the renaissance – was often found outside the city. At some points players within Liverpool could not see a way forward for the problems they were facing. One of the features of Liverpool in the 1980s was the culture of failure that developed as a result of its economic failure, which ate into its politics and psyche. Many of the initiatives that helped to change the city from the 1990s onwards needed a cultural shift, with a different set of attitudes and leaders with a bigger picture about how the place could be changed. It needed someone less involved in the place to propose solutions. A string of government initiatives incentivised local partners to focus on different priorities and challenged Liverpool's leaders to think or behave differently. They attempted to raise aspirations. They all required a degree of confidence that their ambitious targets would be delivered. At the beginning of many of those initiatives it was difficult to imagine that they would succeed. For example, the waterfront was derelict, the city centre was run down, and Speke Garston looked like a failed, outdated industrial and housing estate. But they were radically changed. So initially, it took outsiders with a degree of vision, ambition and confidence both to see and to seize the opportunity. However, Liverpool's leaders themselves became more self-confident as they overcame the culture of failure and successfully delivered key physical and cultural regeneration projects. Delivering Capital of Culture, for example, was crucial to that self-confidence. External intervention – however imperfect and top down – was often a key to the cultural changes that were needed to remake the post-imperial city. It then required local people to respond and deliver. And they did.

Partnership – a cliché but necessary

Partnership has become a much-derided term, often with justification. But it is clear that many of Liverpool's problems stemmed from the confrontational politics that the city endured until the period of normalisation in the 1990s. Relationships between local and national government and between the public and private sectors in Liverpool were strained. And they often made a bad economic situation worse. The era of normalisation was in part intended to reset relationships between the public and private sectors and between national and local government. It was intended to change the role of the local authority from a controlling but inefficient organisation to one that would collaborate with partners to deliver projects and services. Many of the key initiatives were founded on that basis and they did deliver to the city over three decades. The public sector did play a crucial role in Liverpool's renaissance. But the contribution of other partners was crucial at different times. The private sector, which was often absent from the public debate about the city, especially during the difficult economic days of the 1980s and 1990s, has played a more visible and engaged role in its renaissance, even though the multinational companies are not as engaged as they might be and the private sector itself could be more coherently organised. But the Local Enterprise Partnership is one of the largest and best-resourced nationally and it has strengthened its capacity and its relationships with the emerging city regional governance structures. A range of private-sector players

Streets Ahead Festival at night, Sarruga Dracs, dragon sculptures, part of Capital of Culture, 2008
Image reproduced by permission of Culture Liverpool, Liverpool City Council

throughout this story in BOOM, the Mersey Partnership and now the Local Enterprise Partnership have made their contribution as corporate citizens to the Liverpool cause. The private sector still needs to grow and be bigger and more diverse. But its role, contribution and relationships are more significant and more robust now than they once were. The city has learned to work in partnership. Given constraints on public expenditure, this will be more, not less, important in future.

Place-based policy

One of the most obvious features of the Liverpool renaissance is how success came from building particular areas of the city – the waterfront, the city centre, south Liverpool and, more recently, the Knowledge Quarter and the creative and digital Baltic Triangle. Physical renewal in and of itself is not enough. But at times when the challenge of fixing Liverpool seemed overwhelming to many involved, tackling well-defined areas that had some economic potential was one way of achieving progress and developing momentum. There are simple messages about success in such initiatives. They worked best where there was a clear, ambitious, coherent plan from the outset; where government and the local partners worked together; where the public and private sectors were engaged; where there was good political and administrative leadership of a good team; where the area was clearly defined; where significant resources were allocated over a long period of time; where physical, economic and social strategies were adopted; and where need was linked to opportunity. They also underlined the importance of political will, commitment, ambition and leadership. None of this is rocket science. We already have the secrets of success. We know how to do it. But these virtues are often ignored in the search for novelty. And they will be required as Liverpool continues its renaissance in future and addresses the areas of the city that are still to be fixed.

Who made a difference?

Things don't just happen to a city. Someone pulls a lever of some sort – for ill or for good. In the 1980s it was often for ill. But throughout Liverpool's renaissance, it is possible to see the influence of particular individuals who had the confidence and ambition to try to make the city better. The key figure was Michael Heseltine. Despite being from the 'wrong' party, he got, spoke and lobbied for Liverpool, at a time when few other national, and certainly Tory, politicians could or would. Without his policy interventions over three decades, the city would not be the successful, self-confident place it has now become. Many others were identified in the earlier chapters. They came from a variety of sectors and institutions. Some were leaders or chief executives of the city council. Some were chief executives or chairs of regeneration partnerships. Some were the leaders of the government's institutions in the city. Some, if fewer, were from the private sector. At the very dark moments, Liverpool's two great Church leaders made a difference. What these people had was ambition, vision and often courage. They were all personally as much as professionally committed to Liverpool's case. The city captured them and their loyalty – as it has captured many others. They constituted an informal group who worked on many initiatives across the city over a sustained period and built up expertise, understanding, commitment and trust. They shared knowledge, supported each other and influenced local agendas. They were central to the successful delivery by different regeneration organisations. Their values, experience and knowledge were as – if not more – important than institutional mechanisms. More of the same people, trust and capacity will be needed if the city is to continue to flourish. Michael Heseltine's line on this was 'Remember Albert Dock in 1979. Rotting, derelict, toxic, written off. Look at it today. The site is transformed. The city is transformed. The lesson to Liverpool today is that what matters are the person and the people in charge.'[1] You do not have to subscribe to the heroic theory of leadership to see the relevance of that view to Liverpool's long and winding road to renaissance.

What future challenges?

Make devolution deliver

This book has shown that Liverpool has had real success in recent years. But its leaders will have to address many policy challenges in an effort to increase productivity and reduce poverty and inequality in future. Devolution to Liverpool city region could help with this. For example, the city needs to increase the basic skills of many people, either to attract new high-quality jobs to the city region or to give those people a chance of getting such jobs. Placing responsibility for skills with the city region is more likely to deliver those that local employers want. There are too many unemployed people in the city. Devolution will bring more control over the Department of Work and Pension programmes and budgets which could increase the effectiveness of employment programmes and help get people into jobs. Similarly the city region needs to generate about 17,000 new firms to match the national average. Devolution brings greater local control over business services for firms and could help close that gap. The city region needs better, higher-quality, more efficient transport so that people, goods and services can be got into, around and out of the city region more effectively. City regional control over transport could help this. Finally, the city region needs a clearer story about its future development which would outline what kinds of industries will be developed where; where people will live in what kinds of houses; and how they will get from where they live to where they work and play. The new institutional architecture of the city region means that its leaders have an opportunity to write such a narrative.

For this to work, Liverpool leaders will need to sing from a single hymn sheet and put the wider interests of the city region before the interests of particular

parts of it. They will need to make firms and families understand that it is in their interest to operate at city region level, because it will affect their children's opportunities to stay, live, work and play within the city region in future. More hearts and minds have to be won. But that is not a uniquely Liverpool dilemma. All the new post-devolution city regions have had to wrestle with this challenge. And Liverpool is making progress. Since 2017 Liverpool city region has had an elected Labour mayor, Steve Rotheram. This is a new chapter in the Liverpool story with potential to influence its economic trajectory. The mayor's key challenges are self-evident: to get the different parts of the region and the public, private and community sectors engaged; to be the champion for the city region with national government and national and international investors; and to persuade leaders and the public that the city region is a potentially powerful entity which will bring greater economic opportunities to all its people and businesses. Austerity, Brexit and continuing economic uncertainty mean that the job will be more important – if possibly more difficult – in future. At the end of the Metro mayor's first year, when he was essentially setting up his administration and making plans, there was evidence that Rotheram was addressing these issues. He had commissioned some long-term strategic thinking on the low-carbon

CGI image of
Liverpool Waters
Image courtesy
of Peel Land and
Property

and digital economy. He had had some short-term wins. He had invested £30 million in a skills programme, developed a household into work programme, and invested £5 million in cultural programmes. He had committed to a series of big infrastructure projects in the Knowledge Quarter and in Liverpool Waters. He had captured some new money from government, especially for transport and homelessness initiatives. He had increased his capacity to deliver with a growing team of experienced officers and advisers. And despite some hiccups, he had forged better working relationships with the other local authority leaders across the city region, in particular with the elected mayor of Liverpool. Significantly he secured political agreement on the need to create a single agency for attracting investment into and marketing the city region. The first steps on a long journey had been taken.

Internationalise thinking and exploit the global Liverpool brand

'Liverpool's assets are far better than its current brand. So there is huge potential for development.' – Colin Sinclair, director, Knowledge Quarter Liverpool

One of the features of Liverpool's decline as an imperial city was the loss of its internationalist, outward-looking behaviour and attitudes. That is now changing. Being a major player in the Shanghai Expo in 2010 was an important early signal of that. But Liverpool still needs a clearer view of its global role, contribution and significance. In recent years, the city has too narrowly concentrated on its internal affairs, mainly because of the scale of the economic challenges it has faced. But Liverpool's leaders need now to return to their global roots and make wider connections. The city needs to look further forward and outward. The economic debate needs to be more externalised. Liverpool should be more systematic in its international strategy, more consistent and more long term. Liverpool exports far less than might be expected.[2] It has a small number of prime firms that lead exports and it needs to exploit them more for their key international expertise, contacts and supply chains. It needs more collaboration in the way in which different organisations conduct their international business. The city needs to understand better which of its international markets have most potential, in particular whether it is developing markets in Asia or more mature markets in Europe. There are many organisations across the city that already have significant global links – the manufacturing and health-based companies, the universities, the shipping companies, the football clubs. Liverpool needs to deepen and capitalise upon their experience.

Liverpool also needs to improve the way in which it brands itself globally in future.[3] It has seriously underestimated its global significance and appeal and failed to properly exploit it for economic purposes. The city needs a more assertive strategy for capturing the attention of potential international investors. To help do that it needs a compelling shared narrative about its long-term future which it should systematically present globally. That narrative should be bold and ambitious, capturing the city's changed circumstances but rooted in the reality of its current performance on key economic drivers. It should ring true for potential investors, existing businesses, communities, residents, government, students and cultural organisations – locally and globally. It should be future-oriented. If the narrative is to be taken seriously, it should recognise the scale of the city's social challenges rather than ignoring them. It should reflect the city's ambition, scale, transformation, self-confidence, levels of innovation and partnership. It should be about both roots and futures. It should reflect the many past achievements and distinctive features of Liverpool. History matters – but it must not be a prison. The narrative should reflect the extraordinary pace and scale of the changes taking place in the global economy – and show that Liverpool is at the forefront of many of them. It should underline and celebrate the fact that in some globally crucial sectors, Liverpool is a world leader.

'We need to sell the city better than we do. We have to be more outward looking.' – Jim Gill

Go beyond physical regeneration to economic competitiveness
Liverpool's leaders must recognise that the city has gone from one stage of economic development to another, more complex one, and that it will need

different strategies, people and skills in future. The city has been through a very successful period of physical urban regeneration. Given the scale of the economic, institutional and physical problems that the city faced after the decline of the 1970s and 1980s, this was necessary. But while necessary in the past, it will not be sufficient in the future. The city will need to focus on other issues and develop different skills and capacity if it is to sustain its renaissance and compete more effectively nationally and internationally. Its experience in regeneration should not be underestimated. But it will need to operate in a more mature way economically in future. Future growth should be in its known strengths and potential in more advanced markets and products – in the treatment of infectious diseases, advanced manufacturing, logistics and port processing, bio-manufacturing, life sciences and healthcare. It needs to invest more coherently in those sectors and ecosystems. It also needs to explore what more could be done to develop its digital capacity. That is a huge potential market, but despite some known strengths, so far it has remained relatively small and immature in the city. It needs to develop and exploit the economic potential of its low-carbon agenda and plans for tidal energy. In other words, Liverpool needs a plan that continues to capitalise on its regenerated assets and infrastructure and its strengths in the retail, leisure and visitor economy. But it will also have to develop and invest in its high-value-added, knowledge-based assets in future.

Manage political risks

This book has shown how politics, partnership and policy making have changed and improved during the past thirty years and contributed to the continuing renaissance of the city. That overall picture of political progress remains an accurate one. However, politics always changes. For example, the emergence of an elected Metro mayor and city regional governance introduced some new political challenges. Another political concern has been increasingly raised by many people, including those who are centrally involved in local politics and those who are not. Liverpool city and city region are entirely controlled by the Labour Party, so its internal politics have a significant impact on the tone and direction of debate and decision making. The rise of Momentum and the growth in its support has raised challenges for much of the existing political leadership in the city. The movement has demanded more radical policies and has shown considerable discontent with a number of Liverpool MPs in particular. The struggles have been personal and bitter as some MPs' future nominations have been called into question. A number of elected council leaders across the city region are uncertain about the stability of their own leadership as the composition of their party groups in the council shift. The leader of the Wirral local authority gave up under the pressure. The mayor of Liverpool faces a range of internal challenges. Some ward councillors have been deselected and replaced by Momentum members.

Liverpool obviously should welcome robust debate about and challenge to existing policies. There are big questions to be answered about the future direction and development of the city and its economy – and who might benefit and who might not. That debate is necessary. However, concerns have been increasingly raised about whether Momentum's style of politics – and the uncertainty that it might create – might take the city back to the politics of the 1980s, which damaged its reputation nationally and internationally, drove some people out of local politics and deterred some private- and public-sector investment in the city. Local opinion about the implications of current and potential political changes and the level of risk they present is divided. The national political and electoral scene is also unpredictable. The story is still emerging and no one knows how it will develop. But the national Labour leadership needs to better understand the changes that have taken place in Liverpool and do all it can to support the city's continuing renaissance. The question of whether Momentum is – or could become – the new Militant has yet to be answered. But it is a crucial one for everyone in the city to confront.

Share the benefits and spread the wealth of the remade post-imperial city

This book has shown the extent of the renaissance across Liverpool during the past thirty years. Investment and development has continued during the past decade despite austerity. For example, the value and volume of construction in the city centre rose every year from £500 million in 2006 to £1 billion annually in 2015, 2016 and 2017. Between 2012 and 2017 over £5 billion was invested in major capital schemes. The success of this investment is demonstrated by the physical renaissance of the city, the growing numbers of jobs, and the improvement of the public realm. During this period over 9,000 new homes were built. There were 42,000 construction jobs each year. In 2018 there was £1.34 billion of development due for completion by 2021, with two-thirds in the city centre and one-third in the neighbourhoods. Over 5,000 homes were on site, 80% of which were private-sector homes.[4] The city centre and the waterfront have had huge sums of public and private investment and have benefited enormously from them. These areas are clearly among the key drivers of the Liverpool economy, containing crucial parts of, for example, its visitor economy, professional and financial services, retail sector, the knowledge economy and its port and logistics sector.

Equally, there are a series of areas across the city that have the potential to grow and be more successful economically. Typically they are on the fringe of the city centre, which will need to expand, primarily although not exclusively to the north as the existing centre is filled. The key development is Liverpool Waters, Peel Holdings' massive £5.5 billion scheme in the near north docks which is now developing, with a series of residential and office schemes approved and some already built. There are plans to move the existing cruise liner terminal and Isle of Man ferry terminal from near the Pier Head into Liverpool Waters, with a hotel and car parking. There are proposals to

locate Everton football club's new stadium at the top end of the site. Across the road from Liverpool Waters, the city council has launched Ten Streets, a scheme for the regeneration of 125 acres of former dockland intended to create 2,500 new jobs and 1 million sq. ft of development. The aim is to regenerate the northern edge of the city centre and build upon the regeneration of the landmark tobacco warehouse at Stanley Dock into the upmarket Titanic Hotel, and to create a creative and employment district like the Knowledge Quarter and the Baltic Triangle.[5] There are plans to develop the Fabric District on London Road, rescuing the existing furniture and fabric firms but also providing residential and student accommodation, with several schemes already started. But the most important area is the Baltic Triangle, which has become increasingly important in the past decade as a place for creative and digital companies. 4,000 people in over 500 firms in over 30 venues now work in the area in publishing, IT, film, video, advertising, music, graphics, fashion, gaming, software and computer services, cultural and leisure sectors in the three-quarters of a square mile area just on the edge of the traditional retail city centre. There is planning permission for 3,000 new apartments and 500,000 square metres of commercial development. It is attracting increasing international attention and visitors as the new funky part of the city – the digital and creative vanguard of the new Liverpool. The Baltic Quarter is in many ways different from the other places discussed in this book. It is a genuine bottom-up, private-sector-led initiative which has grown organically and which, although originally designated by Liverpool Vision a decade ago, has had very little public or city council support. It is not only where younger industries are developing, it is also where younger people are making an economic contribution to the city. It is a testimony to the new 'Livercool' and the entrepreneurial spirit that is emerging and that will be increasingly needed in future. And that spirit as well as the place and the people should be encouraged and sustained.

'The entrepreneurial spirit in the city is coming back to the fore.' – Councillor Steve Munby

Colourful graffiti in the Baltic Triangle area of Liverpool, created during the Liverpool Street Art Festival
© Ken Biggs/Alamy Stock Photo

These developments underline the pattern that has characterised development in Liverpool since the 1980s, with the slow piecing together of parts of the city as investment and development take place, while other places remain untouched. The city will need to widen and deepen the renaissance that has been taking place and encourage similar growth in those parts of the city that have not yet shared enough in the renaissance of the last decade and a half. Three areas will be crucial to the future of Liverpool. The first is Knowledge Quarter Liverpool on the edge of the city centre, which is an area of enormous economic potential and opportunity. The second area that has to be tackled is north Liverpool, which remains one of the most deprived parts of the UK and which, despite some recent policy initiatives, has not yet fully shared in the city's renaissance. The third is the city centre and waterfront, which has been developed a lot in the past decade but now faces issues of quality and authenticity.

Knowledge Quarter Liverpool – the biggest opportunity for the post-imperial city

Liverpool has world-leading specialisms in infection research, personalised health systems, paediatrics, materials chemistry, sensor technology, sports science, high-performance computing, music, and creative and performing arts. However, until the city region's *Science and Innovation Audit* for national government in 2017, it was not clear that the scale and potential of these sectors had been sufficiently appreciated or integrated into a coherent plan that would provide a clear, long-term investment and development path for them. The audit underlined that the city region already had global strengths in three areas – infection, materials chemistry and high-performance and cognitive computing, underpinned by the Liverpool School of Tropical Medicine, the University of Liverpool, Unilever and Hartree, with huge potential for further development. But it needed a more collective, integrated approach to realise their potential.[6]

Knowledge Quarter Liverpool is an important example of where this is now happening. It is one of the keys to Liverpool's future, which stands at the heart of a wider city region science and innovation ecosystem that stretches from Unilever in Wirral to Hartree Computing Centre at Daresbury in Halton. In a compact area that nevertheless covers 40% of the city centre there is the city's main railway station, four universities, a major hospital, a science park, the Paul McCartney supported Liverpool Institute for Performing Arts, Liverpool City College, major cultural organisations such as the theatres and symphony orchestra, two cathedrals, Georgian housing and a host of independent bars, restaurants and hotels. Knowledge Quarter Liverpool is a powerful partnership between the city council, the universities, the hospitals and cultural institutions. It has developed a masterplan and business development strategy for the area which has begun to have an impact on market perceptions of Liverpool and has attracted significant investment from national and international organisations.

It has key institutions and assets including 54,000 university students. New investments are taking place and there are more ambitious plans for the area. In 2018 over £1 billion of new investment was taking place, with the Royal Liverpool Hospital, the Clatterbridge Cancer Centre, the Liverpool Life Science Accelerator, the Digital Innovation Factory, the Materials Innovation Factory and Sensor City. Liverpool John Moores University is building a new campus at the entrance to the Knowledge Quarter next to Lime Street railway station. There is a further £1 billion investment planned. At the bottom of the area near Lime Street the Knowledge Quarter Gateway is providing student accommodation, retail and hotel facilities. At the top of the Quarter in the new Paddington Village, the Liverpool International College will be built for £35 million, preparing international students to enter the University of Liverpool. The Royal College of Physicians is building its northern headquarters with a state-of-the-art healthy building, the Spine. The Rutherford Cancer Centre is being built for £35 million. Beyond the Knowledge Quarter the again state-of-the-art Alder Hey Children's Hospital was completed for £279 million in 2016. And significant efforts are being made to make Knowledge Quarter Liverpool a proper place where people want to live, work, play and stay, with high-quality buildings and public realm, better connections to the city centre and a new railway station.

Knowledge Quarter Liverpool has the potential to become a leading global innovation district with science innovation, technology, education, medicine and culture combined in a single ecosystem. A decade ago the opportunity was barely

recognised in the city. Five years ago it was simply a report and a prospectus. The area was a hidden jewel in the city until the Mayoral Development Zone focused on it after 2012 and really drew attention to its economic potential. After a variety of slow and false starts, the place and the organisation significantly raised their game. Its development potential was strengthened by the creation of a Joint Partnership Company, Sciontec, that will operate across the whole city region and bring in a major private investor. The Knowledge Quarter Liverpool board is chaired by the vice chancellor of the University of Liverpool, Professor Dame Janet Beer, with Liverpool City Council, Hope Street CIC, the Royal Liverpool Hospital, Liverpool John Moores University and the Liverpool School of Tropical Medicine as board members. It appointed a dynamic chief executive, Colin Sinclair, with experience of marketing, regeneration and property development, and under his leadership it has begun to flourish. It demonstrates belief, investment and genuine global opportunity with increasingly mature governance. Knowledge Quarter Liverpool will be the most significant driver of Liverpool's future economic prosperity. The Liverpool boom of the 1990s and 2000s relied heavily on residential, retail, leisure and tourism. That created jobs and led to growth. Both were welcome. But they were not enough. The next wave of economic development in Liverpool has to be of a higher quality and higher added value. The people and assets of Knowledge Quarter Liverpool and the wider city region ecosystem will be crucial to that.

Fixing north Liverpool – the city's biggest challenge

There are big economic, social and physical problems across the whole of Liverpool which must be tackled in future. They include the outlying ex-council estates, the Granby triangle in Toxteth, the inner suburbs surrounding the city centre – typically pre-1919 housing areas such as Kensington which are still zones of transition – and Garston under the bridge in south Liverpool. In some areas near the city centre there are immigrant groups from a variety of backgrounds trapped in very poor-quality, private rental housing. Many people in these places experience long-term unemployment, poverty and exclusion. They have slightly different characters, circumstances and populations. They have had a variety of regeneration initiatives over the years. But they remain part of Liverpool's 'left behind'. So the city's economic and social challenges are not confined to one part of Liverpool.

Nevertheless the most challenging area of the city is north Liverpool. It is a metaphor for Liverpool's recent development path. Its story is one of exclusion and disconnection. It has been excluded from the economic growth and opportunities in the rest of the city region and disconnected from the core assets that are the area's potential source of renewal. Originally it was at the centre of Liverpool's great port economy from which the city forged its global trading connections and built its wealth and international prestige. So it was the area of the imperial city most badly affected by its fall. It has always been the poorest part of the city and remains so, with higher levels of unemployment and crime and lower levels of health, education and housing than the rest of the city. Its condition did not change significantly during the boom years. Austerity has reinforced its problems.

'It is an unknown city within a city.' – Bob Pointing, former chief executive, North Liverpool Partnership

To illustrate the scale of the challenge in north Liverpool it is worth looking in detail at the condition of Anfield ward, where the globally successful Liverpool FC has been based since 1892. The 14,000 people who live in the ward face huge challenges that are worse than the rest of the city and offer a stark contrast to the world of the football club and its millionaire players with whom they live cheek by jowl. The government's Index of Multiple Deprivation showed that in 2015, one-third of the ward's residents lived in neighbourhoods defined as the most deprived 1% nationally, 83% of them lived in neighbourhoods defined as the most deprived 10% nationally. In Liverpool overall, 45% of residents lived in neighbourhoods defined as the most deprived 10% nationally. Worklessness was 23% in contrast to 14% across the city and 8% nationally. Family income was £21k in comparison with the city average of £27k and the national average of £37k, and was less than half that of the richest ward in the city. 40% of primary school children received free school meals in comparison with 26% across the city and 14% nationally. 58% of residents did not own or have access to a car in comparison with 45% in the city and 25% nationally. 17% were claiming incapacity benefit as opposed to 10% in the city and 6% nationally. 43% of children were in poverty in comparison with 32% in the city and 20% nationally. The average price of housing in the area was £55,000 in comparison with £120,000 across the city and £210,000 nationally. Housing vacancy rates were double the city average. 85% of houses were in the lowest council tax band, in comparison with 60% across the city and 24% nationally. Life expectancy was four years below the city average and six years below the national average. The gap in life expectancy between Anfield and the richest ward in Liverpool was eleven years. 31% of 5 year olds were overweight in comparison with 26% across the city and 22% nationally. 36% of the population had no qualifications, compared with 28% in the city and 22% nationally. 11% had qualifications of NVQ4 or above, in contrast with 22% of the city and 27% nationally. Reading, writing and maths levels were 30% lower than the city and 40% lower than the national average. Crime levels were 10% above the city average and 30% above the national average. There had been little growth in diversity and the population was 93% white.

North Liverpool's failure to share in the city's renaissance has been recognised to some degree. For example, there was a Single Regeneration Budget initiative – the North Liverpool Partnership – for the area from 1996 to 2002. That project did have some success, both physical and economic. In its most visible achievements, it encouraged the conversion by Urban Splash of the Collegiate School into

housing and it obtained a European grant for Liverpool Hope University to locate part of its campus in the area, Hope at Everton. However, these developments were not in the heart of the area but at its extreme edge, nearest the city centre. It also found a site for Liverpool Community College, although again this was not at the heart of but on the opposite edge of the area. It helped to reduce unemployment from 36% to 16%, got 1,900 adults into employment, often in the city centre tourist economy, improved the numbers getting five GCSE passes up to 18%, even though this remained low, developed 50% of the derelict land in its area, attracted 150 new, sometimes community, businesses and leveraged in £60 million of private-sector investment. It supported the Housing Action Trust which demolished some of the most undesirable high-rise blocks – the so-called piggeries – in Everton. And it continued the work of the MDC on the arterial routes along the docks, grant-aiding environmental improvements and business expansion. It commissioned feasibility studies for projects that happened later such as the conversion of the Stanley Dock warehouse into the Titanic Hotel.

Given the scale of the problems it faced, its limited resources and the uncertain start it endured, the Partnership delivered some change in the area. But it could never deliver the ambitious targets it had set itself in order to win government funding, which were unrealistic. Similar initiatives in different places delivered better results for their resources. Why? The Partnership was troubled by community conflicts and disagreements. It did not spend enough money or deliver enough projects at the beginning and it was yellow carded by government for underperformance half way through its life. The original chief executive was removed at that point and the Partnership had to be reconstructed. It also had a regular turnover of board chairs. It was better at engaging and dealing with the community than with the local private sector, which was often deterred from getting involved by the area's complex and febrile community politics. The Partnership might have been expected to be a way of overcoming those differences. Instead it became an arena within which local rivalries, arguably a residue of older sectarian divisions but also of the competition for casual jobs in the docks that had traditionally divided individuals, families and streets, were played out. And the scale of the resources – £22.5 million for six years – could not touch the scale of need, given the area's size and the structural changes that it had gone through. At the end of the initiative, as a senior policy maker put it, 'the same old issues were trundling on and many of the same characters were still in place'. Whatever its achievements or limitations, one of the problems was that after 2002 the initiative was ended.

'It was not coordinated and it was not followed up. There was no overarching strategy.' – Bob Pointing

The same thing happened to the next big plan for the area, the Housing Market Renewal Pathfinder. This was created under the Labour government in 2007 to tackle failed housing markets across the city. But it was stopped just as it got going by the change in government in 2010. The money was cut off and the project never really delivered what had been intended. Parts of the area remained half knocked down and half rebuilt for several years. Despite differences of opinion about the HMRP strategy and the scale of demolition that was needed in the area, it still has far too much inadequate, pre-1919 terraced housing.

In 2010 there was another initiative for the area. A joint Liverpool and Sefton City Council *Strategic Regeneration Framework for North Liverpool* was adopted.[7] This provided a good analysis of the nature and scale of the problem. It identified some important principles that should govern the effort to regenerate the area. It made plans for some projects. And there has been progress on some of these projects, especially around the Liverpool football stadium. But again there was not enough policy substance at the end of the analysis. It did not create a properly resourced delivery vehicle with a clear plan and the political and administrative clout to make the scale of the changes necessary.

'The framework, rather like the one for the city centre, is kept on the shelf. But it does not influence our daily activities. It is rolled out to justify individual development decisions.' – Ged Fitzgerald

A key question is why this happened and why north Liverpool has been allowed to face such challenges for so long. The failure to systematically address the problem is arguably a stain on the city's conscience. Of course, many of the problems faced by the area and its people are the consequences of changes in the wider world

Boys playing in Everton Park as it was being built, with the Braddocks behind them, 1985
© Dave Sinclair

and external economy. The collapse of the port and its related activities such as sugar processing at Tate and Lyle had a devastating impact on the area, which depended on the jobs and the income the port provided. It paid a heavy price for the decline of the imperial economy. Also, Liverpool is not unique in struggling to raise aspirations and performance in areas where there have been long-standing economic problems, often with families who have experienced three generations of unemployment. These are the wicked issues facing many cities in a de-industrialising global economy. But more has been done in similar places in Liverpool itself, so this structural explanation is not enough.

A number of explanations have been offered. Partly they concern the nature of the place. North Liverpool's imperial economy was insecure, with very low-skilled casual employment in the docks and dockside processing which provided little opportunity to build a skills base. Also, despite the important Everton Park and revitalised Stanley Park, it is physically challenging, with few green areas and predominantly pre-1919 housing and declining small shops. It is also a very large and mixed area with a large dockland, much run-down nineteenth-century terraced housing, some modern council and privatised housing estates and a visible and influential community-based housing association – the Eldonian Village – in the middle.

'It is a way of getting into Liverpool more than a place. The links are north–south when they should be east–west. This underlines the fragmentation of the area and the lack of sense of unity of purpose.' – Alan Chape

The area has been physically destroyed twice in recent memory – once by the Luftwaffe in the Second World War and then again by the planners in the 1960s, who moved people and communities out of the area to the estates on the periphery of the city – which themselves subsequently declined. The development that did take place was low quality with little green space. The creation of Everton Park in the middle of it in the 1980s provided welcome green space but it also contributed to physical dislocation and gaps between different communities in the area. It helped to break the community bonds that are necessary for social cohesion and diminished the pool of civic activism. In the words of Ian Wray, former chief planner for the Northwest Development Agency, all this 'undermined the creation of consensual social institutions which spoke for all – at a level above the street block but below the whole city'.

It can also be argued that there has never been an effort to address the challenges of north Liverpool in a sustained coherent way, as was done in Speke Garston in the south of the city in the 1990s. As we saw earlier, the initiatives there made a real difference to the place and its people. However, Speke Garston, whatever its problems, was an easier task. It had more economic assets, activity, potential and anchor institutions than north Liverpool. Also, a key policy difference between north Liverpool and Speke Garston was that, although they both had regeneration partnerships addressing the social challenges of the area, Speke Garston also had a powerful, well-resourced economic development company. This dealt with the economy of the area and could link opportunity and growth to poor communities. North Liverpool did not. Its focus was on the social challenges, and they were too deep for the partnership mechanism to deal with. The arrangements were trying to patch up the people but not tackling the underlying economic challenges. In the words of Alan Chape, 'It skimmed across the surface of the problems. It could never get under and dig into them.' So north Liverpool did not undergo the scale of transformation achieved in Speke Garston in the 1990s. And twenty years later the gap between the two areas looks even greater.

In part the area's problems were so great that it was easier to work on other parts of the city that promised greater or earlier success for policies and politicians. Community politics in north Liverpool are complex, often divisive and challenging to manage. In part it was a failure of political commitment, leadership, ambition or vision. It has been argued that there were not enough votes in north Liverpool to get political attention. In particular, some argued that the Liberal Democrats' natural base was in south Liverpool, so they paid less attention to the north.

'We were seen as an old Labour Partnership by the Liberal Democrats. I felt denuded of resources and political support from the council leadership.' – Bob Pointing

The Merseyside Development Corporation (MDC) did have powers and resources and responsibility for part of north Liverpool and was making a physical and economic impact in the dockland part of the area. But it was closed down by government in 1997. That was too soon in some people's eyes. Overall, in the words of John Flamson, 'We were playing at it. We needed a new model of leadership – but we got the same old.'

However, the most important problem of the area is that there are very few if any large employers or anchor institutions that have a stake there. Many of the large firms such as Tate and Lyle were lost in the 1980s. The Mersey Docks and Harbour Company had never been an enlightened employer in the area before it went out of business. There were no leading hospitals, schools or colleges. The exceptions were Everton and Liverpool football clubs – major national and global institutions located in a hard-pressed community. However, at least historically, the football clubs did not recognise the extent to which they could and should be involved in the economic and social affairs of their surrounding neighbourhoods. Changes in ownership and uncertainty about its long-term development plans prevented Liverpool football club from playing a major part before the current owners took over in 2010. As a senior policy maker said of the club in the first decade of this century, 'It dithered and blighted the area.'

Now both clubs and their new chief executives have recognised and are committed to changing that position and are supporting a wide range of employment, social and educational initiatives – necessarily, but sadly, including food banks. Everton in the Community has done a huge amount of community and volunteering work and invested over £9 million in recent years in buildings and facilities in the area. In the words of Richard Kenyon of Everton in the Community, 'We have virtually replaced the local authority because it has no resources for the area.' The club is adamant that if it moves its stadium to Liverpool Waters, it will leave a significant community legacy rather than abandoning the residents. Similarly, the Anfield Project – a partnership between the city council, Your Housing group and Liverpool FC which started in 2012 – is a £260 million regeneration scheme which will create 1,000 new homes and rebuild community and retail facilities by 2018 around Liverpool's football stadium. A lot of progress has been made since the plan was devised in 2010, with the renewal and expansion of Anfield stadium, the refurbishment of some of the nearby Edwardian terraces and a series of new-build houses. Stanley Park has been carefully restored, and there are plans to revitalise the main high street that passes Anfield. Project Rosemary is another part of the 2010 plan which has brought physical regeneration to the Scotland Road area, including an upmarket supermarket. There are also schemes to raise educational aspirations and performance in the area. The LFC Foundation undertakes important community and volunteering work with the community. The University of Liverpool with the Foundation has launched the IntoUniversity scheme designed to raise the aspirations and achievements of local school children.

There is greater optimism in north Liverpool to match the greater commitment of the local authority and the football clubs. There is demonstrable progress on

the ground. But neither the residents, the football clubs nor the local authority believe that they have done more than start the process of regeneration. Despite the evident physical progress in parts of the area, this part of the challenge of remaking the post-imperial city not yet been met. Levels of educational aspiration and attainment, employment, health, income and investment will all have to be raised in future. As the football clubs become even more financially successful and even bigger players on a global stage, the opportunity for investment in them will inevitably increase. But there is a risk that this could increase the contrast with their immediate surroundings. The centre of gravity of Liverpool is moving northwards. The success of the Stanley warehouse regeneration because of the Titanic Hotel, the developments now taking place in Liverpool Waters and the plans for the Ten Streets area make growth and investment in the area inevitable. When that does happen it is crucial that some of the jobs and wider social opportunities go to local people in and around Anfield and Everton – otherwise it will increase rather than reduce concerns about social justice and cohesion in post-imperial Liverpool.

'The gap is just too much. There could be gated communities in north Liverpool – with a few inside and the rest locked out.' – Alan Chape

North Liverpool needs a new approach. Arguably the city missed an opportunity when New Labour was in power and David Miliband was willing to support a

Aerial view of Liverpool FC's Anfield stadium looking across Stanley Park to Everton FC's Goodison Park
© A.P.S. (UK)/Alamy Stock Photo

major initiative for the area. Government officials suggested either extending Liverpool Vision to the area or creating an urban regeneration, development or neighbourhood company. At that time the local authority did not respond sufficiently positively to the opportunity and was more interested in the amount of money it would get rather than the strategic opportunity to work with government. 'They said everything was in hand and so lost the chance of doing something on the scale needed. The Minister could not take them seriously', a senior civil servant observed. That moment, opportunity and resources have gone. But the city must now ask whether a powerful partnership organisation between the key institutions with resources and a long-term remit for the area would help make sure that north Liverpool gets its fair share in future. Here, twenty years' experience of successful regeneration schemes in many other parts of the city is relevant. Such schemes worked when they commanded political and policy attention. Many of the areas involved seemed beyond recovery. But when there was the ambition, the vision, the leadership and the political will to regenerate them it did happen. The same is now needed for north Liverpool.

It is currently designated as a Mayoral Development Zone, but this does not have the levers, resources or capacity to deliver what is needed. There needs to be a partnership that comprises the key players that are currently working in and with the firms and people in the area, including at least the two football clubs, Peel Holdings, the city council, the universities and Liverpool City College. Others could be added. That organisation needs to have the resources, commitment and capacity to take at least a twenty-year view of the area and to deliver the key economic, social, educational and physical changes that will be needed to end its exclusion and disconnection. Such a model has been adopted in Knowledge Quarter Liverpool with some success. It is well resourced and well governed and has a sophisticated economic development strategy that combines economic analysis, place marketing, place making and connectivity. If it is good enough for the potential future economic driver of Liverpool, some version of it should be good enough for north Liverpool so that the city can get on and deliver on its inclusive growth agenda. In fact it could be argued that north Liverpool is more than a city issue. It crosses the boundaries of two local authorities. The scale is so large and the impact of the challenge so great that it could be a city regional priority as well. The physical changes and the investment that will inevitably take place in north Liverpool should be a catalyst and incentive to tackle and finance the community regeneration that is still desperately needed. The balance between sustaining the existing community and diversifying it with new activities and people will have to be carefully addressed.

'Carrying on as we are now will not address the problems or the perception of the area – nor provide the glue to bind together the various factions and interests.' – John Flamson

A booming city centre – the quality of the development of the post-imperial city

For thirty years Liverpool city centre paid the price for the city's economic failure. Paradoxically, the recovery of the city's economy and the scale, pace and quality of the development of the city centre has raised questions about the potential price of economic success. City leaders in future will have to walk a tightrope and balance the need for development, growth and investment with the need to preserve what is unique and special about Liverpool's place quality. There are concerns that its special characteristics may be at risk because of the quality of some of the development as well as some of the leisure and visitor offer, which is near the bottom of the market. The city needs to balance volume with quality, otherwise everywhere in the city centre could suffer.

UNESCO and the World Heritage site saga

The general issue about the pace and nature of city centre development was most dramatically raised in 2017 in a very public controversy about the possibility that, because of potential overdevelopment, Liverpool could lose its World Heritage status which had been granted by UNESCO in 2004. At that time, large parts of the dockland and the commercial and cultural areas of the city centre were

Liverpool waterfront with the city behind, 2015
© Paul White – North West England/Alamy Stock Photo

designated with the status of a Maritime Mercantile City.[8] But its status was called into question after the city council gave outline planning consent for the development of the near north docks to its new owners, Peel Holdings. Peel's original ambitions were to create a Shanghai on the Mersey, with considerable development, high densities and large numbers of high-rise buildings. UNESCO was alarmed by the proposed developments and in 2011 Liverpool was placed on the 'at risk' register and asked to clarify but also importantly to change its policies for development. UNESCO wanted a moratorium placed on all development on the site until the city council had given a satisfactory account of the proposed developments and had met its concerns. The proposal to build Everton football stadium at the edge of the World Heritage site ramped up the concerns and confusion even further. The issue rumbled on until 2017 when the city was given a final warning by UNESCO and a further year to act before it was de-listed. It became a very visible and contentious issue both within the city and nationally, with conflicting arguments between the various groups including the mayor, the council, the owners, the developers, the media and conservation groups. The debate was heated, with claims and counter-claims about what Liverpool already had and had not done, what it was proposing to do and what risks it posed to the different parts of the Maritime Mercantile City and its World Heritage status.

This being Liverpool, the story was complicated, but several points were clear. First, Liverpool had a very good case to make about the level of investment it had made in its historic and heritage assets, retrieving many from disrepair and reducing the number of derelict heritage buildings in the city centre to below 3%. But the city had not promoted its achievements clearly enough. Secondly, despite this investment, Liverpool had not sufficiently developed or promoted its World Heritage status and had made less of it than other UK cities such as Edinburgh or Bath. It was a missed opportunity. Thirdly, the city had not responded positively or constructively enough to UNESCO's concerns over several years. It had not made its position sufficiently clear. Fourthly, the owners, Peel Holdings, had not done enough either to develop or publicise a coherent vision for the near north docks which could reassure UNESCO about the quality of the planned developments. Finally, UNESCO and its World Heritage committee was a classic international organisation and not the easiest to deal with. So there was blame all round.

Underlying the debate was the alleged conflict between conservation and development in the city centre. The political leadership and the mayor in particular were adamant that having had forty years of decline, Liverpool needed growth and development to become sustainable again. In particular it needed development in the near north docks if prosperity was ever going to return to north Liverpool, the most deprived part of the city and one of the most deprived parts of the UK. The mayor was not willing to let concerns about the loss of World Heritage status put that development at risk. In fact, it was clear that conservation and development were not necessarily in conflict and that improved relationships and decision making should be able to resolve the issue and avoid Liverpool losing its World Heritage status.

After a period of megaphone diplomacy and provocative national and international news stories in the summer of 2017, the mayor decided to defuse the issue and appointed a Special Task Force to advise him on the future of the World Heritage site. The work of this group led the mayor and the city council to adopt a more nuanced position. The leadership admitted that it had not made the best case on behalf of the city to UNESCO. It also recognised that the city had not made enough of the asset of World Heritage status and that it had rather been overtaken by the excitement of winning the Capital of Culture bid at the same time in 2004. It offered to rectify this by setting up a charitable trust to make much more of the site in future. It also offered to extend its boundaries to take in parts of the city that probably should have been designated in the first instance. Most significantly, Peel Holdings substantially revised their plans. This was partly in the light of changing market needs and partly out of recognition that such an extraordinary waterfront required a more place-based approach that reflected the significance of the site, the quality of the water space and also connected better with communities outside the World Heritage site in the Ten Streets and the successful regeneration of Stanley Dock. Peel produced a more expansive, rounded set of development proposals with more parkland, lower densities and fewer tall buildings. In 2018 these combined measures earned Liverpool a reprieve and at the UNESCO meeting in Bahrain the city was given another year to develop its proposals before it lost its listed status. That story is still unfolding but there is optimism that the status will be retained. However, questions about the quality of development in the city centre still face the city.

Looking ahead – what kind of Liverpool for whom in future?

This book has looked at key events, decisions and actions that have shaped Liverpool's development in the past thirty years. But it has raised a question about the future as well as the recent past of the city. At this point that question should be obvious. It is – what kind of city should be created for whom in future? In turn this raises three strategic challenges of productivity, people and place.

What kind of economy? More productive with more and better jobs

This book has rehearsed the many achievements of the Liverpool economy during the past two decades. It should build on those achievements and assets. Elsewhere I have called them 'Boats, Beatles, Brains and Barrage'.[9] They are what Liverpool already has, is known for and is good at. The boats are the port and logistics. The Beatles are the cultural, creative, sporting and digital industries. The brains are the educational and research organisations driving the knowledge economy of Liverpool city region. The barrage is the potential of the river Mersey to generate greener, more sustainable energy. To this could be added cars, chemicals and cash (or financial services). There is huge future opportunity to exploit all these assets further. But this book has also shown the challenges Liverpool faces and where it must do better. There are some processes that it must continue to improve. Its leaders must continue to develop trust and more robust working relationships between the public and private sectors. They also need to generate and promote a clearer economic narrative about the future. Importantly, despite the continuing importance of the public sector in the city, Liverpool will need to go even more with the grain of the market and depend less upon declining public resources in future. It will need to grow its private sector. It will also need to improve its productivity. This is a national and not simply a local problem, but it is a particularly big challenge for Liverpool. At its simplest, Liverpool needs more people in more productive jobs – and more existing or new businesses to create those jobs. If it can grow the number of firms, increase its investment in skills and infrastructure and build upon the example of the many successful firms already in Liverpool, it will increase its productivity and grow its economic pie.

As we have seen, the productivity of Liverpool's residents is lower than many other cities but the productivity of its workers is higher. This is because some sectors of the Liverpool economy, especially in advanced manufacturing – including automobiles, chemicals and pharmaceuticals – are very successful and productive. In these sectors investment has been high and skills are high, even though they are capital- rather than labour-intensive and do not employ large numbers of people. Their productivity underlines the need to attract and develop these kinds of firms. It also underlines the need to improve the skills of the city's people so they can get these jobs when they are created – or to help attract such firms and investment in the first place. Of course, not all jobs can or should be in these highly productive sectors. Existing jobs in other sectors will remain important sources of employment and income. But increasing productivity in all sectors of Liverpool's economy will be crucial, and will make the city better able to pay for the things it wants to and must do to improve the conditions of both the place and its people.

What about the people? A fairer and more equal city

Liverpool has had and is having an extraordinary renaissance. There are a huge number of good things to build upon. The people of Liverpool are proud of what they and their city have achieved. The city looks, feels and is better in many ways. But renaissance is not only about places, it is about people – and all the people. The question that raises its head at the end of this story is: has enough yet been done for or delivered to all the people of the city? It is fair to say that the answer is not yet. Liverpool is the fourth most-deprived local authority in England, and 45% of the city's neighbourhoods are among the 10% most deprived in England. In 2017 over 32,000 were in poverty and in two wards the rate was over 50%. 1,200 children were in local authority care – higher than similar cities. Life expectancy was six years below the England average. It lagged behind the nation in both school readiness and educational attainment. 23% of its resident workers earned below the real living wage. 13% of its residents were not working because of long-term illness. There were fewer of the very deprived in 2015 than there were in the Index of Multiple Deprivation of 2007. But the numbers in the next most deprived sector remain largely untouched. What this means in practice to peoples' lives is movingly shown in *Getting By*, a study of 30 working Liverpool families.[10]

The scale of the social challenge in Liverpool is shown in Maps 3 and 4, which are based on the government's Index of Multiple Deprivation reports of 2007 and 2015. Map 3 shows the extent of deprivation across the city in 2015. It is concentrated in north Liverpool, although as we said earlier, parts of Garston and Toxteth are also particularly deprived. The south and the city centre are the least deprived parts of Liverpool. The south has always been comfortable and the city centre has had the bulk of policy attention and investment, as this book has shown. The map also shows that the gap between the most and least deprived areas of the city is very large. And it underlines that a significant number of neighbourhoods concentrated in Everton and Anfield are in the most deprived 1% of all neighbourhoods nationally.

Map 3. Liverpool,
2015: most
deprived places
and people
(Crown Copyright,
2018)

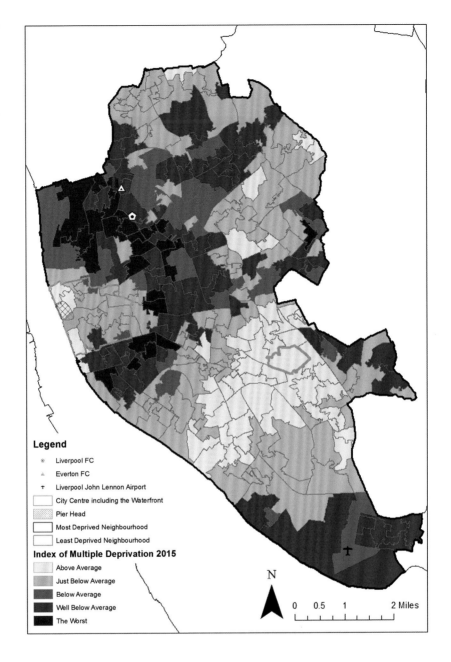

Legend

- ⊙ Liverpool FC
- ⌂ Everton FC
- ✝ Liverpool John Lennon Airport
- ☐ City Centre including the Waterfront
- ▨ Pier Head
- ☐ Most Deprived Neighbourhood
- ☐ Least Deprived Neighbourhood

Index of Multiple Deprivation 2015

- Above Average
- Just Below Average
- Below Average
- Well Below Average
- The Worst

N

0   0.5   1   2 Miles

Map 4 presents even more challenging evidence. It shows how different parts of the city fared during the period of austerity 2007–15. The north of the city remained pretty much where it was in terms of deprivation, even though the numbers of the most deprived fell a little. However, the south got better, with the biggest improver improving its status in the national picture by almost 25%. In other words the gap between the poor and rich parts of Liverpool is not only big, it is growing.

It is crucial that policies are put in place to make sure that those who did not benefit during the boom are not left further behind in the bust. This is not

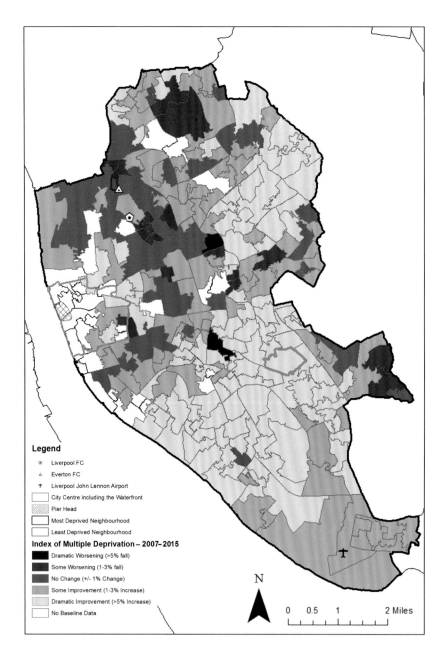

Map 4. Liverpool in austerity, 2007–15: who and where won and lost? (Crown Copyright, 2018)

Legend

⊕ Liverpool FC

⌂ Everton FC

✝ Liverpool John Lennon Airport

☐ City Centre including the Waterfront

▨ Pier Head

☐ Most Deprived Neighbourhood

☐ Least Deprived Neighbourhood

Index of Multiple Deprivation – 2007–2015

■ Dramatic Worsening (>5% fall)

■ Some Worsening (1-3% fall)

■ No Change (+/- 1% Change)

■ Some Improvement (1-3% Increase)

☐ Dramatic Improvement (>5% Increase)

☐ No Baseline Data

N

0   0.5   1   2 Miles

a uniquely Liverpool problem, but is a challenge for cities and governments nationally and globally. Nor is it a new problem. I wrote thirty years ago about the first Massachusetts miracle that the 'fruits of prosperity in Boston had not been evenly shared'.[11] Thirty years later the same is true of Liverpool's growing prosperity. So in the next part of its story Liverpool must focus unrelentingly on making the city better for all of its people. Inclusive growth is now the mantra locally and nationally. Like partnership, it is another cliché. But it is equally true. Liverpool City Council has just endorsed it and produced a large action plan to address it.[12] It is a central plank of the Metro mayor's and the city region's new investment strategy. It is important that in the next decade they – and other organisations in the city – start to deliver on it. It will not be simple, straightforward or quick, as the review by Sissons et al. of the lack of progress across city regions nationally on this issue, despite devolution, shows.[13] But it is needed. And the lessons of the past thirty years are that the city, its leaders and people can achieve great things when they set their minds to it. They need to do this again on this great challenge.

What kind of place? Quality and authenticity

At the beginning of this book I wrote that Liverpool was not better than other cities, but that it was different. That difference is one of its key assets and advantages and it is important that the difference is nourished in future, and not overwhelmed by too much or the wrong kind of development. Authenticity, quality and character will be the keys to Liverpool city centre's future success. The World Heritage site debate raised this more general issue about future development in the city and the need not only to maintain momentum during a period of austerity, but to achieve the quality of development that would be an asset in the longer term. There are concerns that development across the city has not been sufficiently coherent and too many buildings have not been of the right quality. The city has changed, with different parts flourishing in different ways at different times for different markets. The waterfront is a good example of this. It is the jewel in Liverpool's crown and has developed extraordinarily during the past decade. But there now needs to be a more coherent approach to the relationship between it and the city centre. It should be better integrated with the area across the Strand, the highway that divides the two sectors. The retail and leisure offer needs to be more systematically managed and improved so that the museums, independent shops, bars and restaurants in the different parts of the city centre become a more integrated attractive offer for leisure and business visitors and local people.

Given the global iconic significance of the Liverpool waterfront, it needs to be governed or managed in a more coherent way. No organisation has the right capacity, powers and resources to ensure that the quality of development will be high enough in future. There has been a phase of significant but ad hoc development up and down the waterfront. There are a variety of organisational fingers in the waterfront pie. A more strategic, long-term view needs to be taken of the whole area, which stretches several miles from the part-derelict but huge opportunity of the original International Garden Festival site in the south, through the Albert Dock area in the centre, to the near north docks and Liverpool Waters, up to the proposed development of Everton football stadium at Bramley Moore Dock.

'Liverpool is an incredible place to invest for industries to whom place matters.' – Jon Hague, Unilever and LCR LEP

The quality of its development in the next decade will be an important part of Liverpool's economic attractiveness in the longer term. The city has gone beyond the point of being a willing victim for developers and is now at the stage where it should expect to demand higher quality from them. Changes in national policy mean that the planning system no longer puts the quality of development above the cost of development. So quality is underplayed. But there is still scope and indeed a need for the political leadership of the city to set high standards and encourage future developers and developments that meet the city's long-term aspirations. This is related to the argument about the kind of place Liverpool wants to be, the product it wants to promote and the kind of visitors it wants to attract. For example, there is a risk of going too far downmarket in the search for visitors. Some parts of the city centre, especially at weekends, are in danger of becoming a victim of their own success. When the city centre had its real growth in the first decade of the century there was an economic development narrative provided by Liverpool Vision's regeneration framework. Liverpool needs a similar narrative now, which links the development of individual sites and buildings to wider place-making issues as well to the emerging needs of the city's future economy. The city's Strategic Investment Framework, written in 2012, does not fully do that job.[14] If the city wants to be attractive for investors and visitors in twenty years' time, it needs to start making the decisions now that will make sure this happens. The city should consider creating an independent organisation with world-leading members whose remit should be to directly confront such place-making issues and put quality and authenticity of place as key criteria for future development. Liverpool is rightly no longer an imperial city, but its reputation means that it remains a truly global one. Its aspirations and ambitions for the quality of the place should match this. And it could build into this vision equally ambitious targets to be green, clean and sustainable. The city now, as I said of Liverpool Vision and the city centre at the beginning of the twenty-first century, should 'Make no small plans'.

There are also big questions about the future of housing in the city centre and whether there is enough family accommodation being built as opposed to apartments for younger, single people and students. There is no denying that there is a real need for higher value housing in the city in future for both financial and economic reasons. Financially, one of the local authority's key problems is that a very high percentage of its housing stock is of lower value, and so does not generate enough income from council tax. This worsens the impact of austerity and declining financial support from government. The city needs a better mix of housing types with more of higher value to generate the council taxes to pay for the city's public services in future. But in addition to financial considerations a more diverse mix of properties is also important for the city's future economic development. There is still a massive over-supply of inadequate, pre-1919 property across the city that existing residents don't want. And there is a shortage of higher-quality housing to attract the kind of workers that Liverpool's economy will need in future. The city still has a large amount of land that could be filled with housing. It certainly has not reached the situation of London, where critics argue that development and regeneration have become essentially gentrification and social and ethnic cleansing. Liverpool is a long way from that. But the right balance still has to be found.

Liverpool's economy will be different in ten years' time and the character and quality of the city centre needs to anticipate and reflect this. For example, the digital and creative sectors of the economy will clearly grow and it is important that the right kind of provision is made for them in future. But it is also important that the existing parts of the city that they occupy are protected from standard commercial overdevelopment. In some cases in the Baltic Triangle, the most developed and mature of these areas, that risk has already been realised through demolition and development. These enterprises and activities should not be priced out of the city centre because that will lead to a loss of both economic opportunity and cultural diversity. They, like the cultural institutions in the city, make Liverpool a more interesting city to live, work, visit and potentially invest in. So Liverpool leaders must avoid squeezing them out and creating a homogeneous city centre dominated by retail and leisure.

It is also important that already successful and newly emerging areas such as the Baltic Triangle,[15] the Ten Streets Quarter[16] and the Fabric District are seen as a connected economy and not simply as disconnected buildings and development sites. That would be a missed opportunity. They are part of an ecosystem that should be nourished. Equally, those sites and sectors should have a clearer relationship with Knowledge Quarter Liverpool. As a Mayoral Development

Liverpool waterfront from the air showing The Strand, which separates the city from the waterfront, 2017
© Paul White – North West England/Alamy Stock Photo

Zone it is different in scale, resources and governance terms from these smaller places. But it has similar strategic economic ambitions and is physically very close to all of them. They should be better connected. The city needs to think more strategically about what it is doing and what it should be doing in these creative areas. It needs a more sophisticated development strategy that will reflect the needs and opportunities of the next decade rather than the one that worked in the first decade of this century, which essentially involved physical regeneration. There are great gains to be made here by joining up the dots. But that conversation is not yet taking place consistently enough between the policy makers and the firms that are driving that part of the economy.

So what for whom?

So what for government? More commitment to cities is needed

The story of Liverpool speaks to something bigger nationally. The most obvious point about the city's fall and renaissance over thirty years is that they coincided with either the withdrawal of government attention, support and resources for cities, or with greater attention, support and resources for them. The Thatcher government's policy in the 1980s to reduce public expenditure and support for local authorities created huge financial problems for Liverpool which fed into its politics and compounded its woes, including the Toxteth riots. By contrast, the city had its most successful period when a New Labour government after 1997 was committed to intervening and funding regeneration initiatives. In fact, this is part of a more general pattern of city development in the UK. It was not only Liverpool that benefited from government support at that time. Equally, Liverpool's challenges have grown again under austerity since 2010, as government has retreated from its commitment to cities. The government's policies have created huge fiscal challenges for the city's leadership. Those policies are encouraging a capital-rich but revenue-poor, increasingly divided city, with private development for better-off places and people and squeezed public services for poorer places and people. That simply cannot be right or fair.

More generally, despite its devolution initiatives and plans to develop national and local industrial strategies, government has withdrawn from a coherent urban or regeneration policy. This simply no longer exists in the UK. Even the devolution and Northern Powerhouse agenda that flourished after 2012 has lost significant impetus, as the cast of characters in government changed and its architects and supporters – David Cameron, George Osborne, Michael Heseltine and Jim O'Neill – lost their grip on power. This risks increasing the already large gap between the north and south as public and private investment and attention goes to London and the south-east at the expense of the north. A clear example of this is differential infrastructure investment in the south as opposed to the north, where the investment bar is placed higher. Specifically, Liverpool, in not being directly connected to HS2, combined with the government's failure to electrify the rail system across the north, will pay a heavy price for this bias in national attention and investment. It will be held back by national policy. As my review of the wider European experience in *Second Tier Cities* showed, more successful cities lead to better balanced and more successful national economies. There is an economic as well as a moral case for investing in cities beyond the capital, even in austerity. The Liverpool story has demonstrated that public expenditure when regarded as investment does create national and local benefits. Government would be wise to recognise its own self-interest, let alone the interests of cities like Liverpool. The lesson from Liverpool is that government has done, can do and should be doing more not less with and for our cities.

What messages for the influencers? Come and see the truth

I said at the beginning of *Liverpool on the Brink* that Liverpool is a test case of how the country responds to urban challenges. But Liverpool itself has also responded – and its culture and performance have changed. The city and its people have been resilient in adversity. The long campaign to get justice for the victims of Hillsborough underlined its commitment to demonstrating the truth about that event. It was a tragedy that speaks to the character of the city and its people. Just as the truth about that day was finally spoken, it can be argued that the truth about the city itself is also being spoken. But that truth is not yet totally heard or accepted. I said at the start of this book that cultural blindness and almost casual racism have characterised some national portrayals of Liverpool. The newspaper headline 'No good can come out of Liverpool' was as unfair and untrue then as it is now. But a degree of ignorance about the city's recent changes

Vigil at St George's Hall, Liverpool, 27 April 2016, in memory of the 96 who were killed in the 1989 Hillsborough tragedy and subsequently absolved of any blame
© WENN Ltd/Alamy Stock Photo

and achievements remains – more at home than abroad. Those stereotypes need to be dismissed. The truth about the city is self-evident. It is not perfect and it is not finished. But its people, organisations and leaders have helped to remake it. There is real evidence to challenge the tired clichés about Liverpool that are still occasionally found among the media, the political class and the investor class. The city must consistently make that challenge. The most common observation about the city is that when people actually come and see it, they are 'gobsmacked'. Liverpool needs more people, media, politicians and investors to come and see what has happened and is happening. If they do, many will end up supporting, staying in or investing in the city. And that would encourage a more successful and balanced set of cities in this country – which would be very good for UK PLC.

So what for other places?

Liverpool is not just a local story about a city going through a renaissance. It stands for something more important. The key message of the past thirty years is that even the most unpromising places and economies can be turned round. It was not obvious thirty years ago that renaissance was possible in Liverpool. It took a lot of time, effort, commitment, faith, imagination and money. It took bravery, confidence and ambition. It involved building on what it was good at and known for, but also seizing new opportunities along the way. It involved many

Cityscape
© McCoy Wynne
(mccoywynne.co.uk)

visible and less visible people, locally, nationally and from Europe. There were disappointments as well as successes along the way. There were deep lows as well as huge highs. There was not a single or simple script. Luck played a part, for good or ill. As the UK in its post-Brexit days starts to worry about the smaller, 'left behind' places outside the cities, we should not forget the importance to the future of the national economy of the big cities such as Liverpool nor underestimate the relevance or value of its renaissance to other places. Liverpool is different. But its experience shows what is possible. Its story should give hope and encouragement to many similar places in the UK and beyond

So what for the Scousers?

'When Michael Heseltine used to visit the city in the 80s everyone would come up and ask him what he was going to do to help Liverpool. Now everyone comes up to tell him what they are doing to help Liverpool. We have taken responsibility for and ownership of our place and its future.'
– Mark Basnett

The most important message of this book is for the people, businesses and leaders of Liverpool. The city has turned the corner. It is not going back to the bad old days, even if it has more challenges ahead. The qualities it has shown recently

of increasing confidence, ambition, leadership, partnership, trust and delivery will serve it better than the pessimism and introversion of the culture of failure that developed during the dark and difficult days of the 1980s. There is more to be done. However, much – although not all – of it is the hands of Liverpool's leaders. They will need to define, drive and deliver a more successful future with increased productivity, higher place quality and fairer shares of success. They will need to take a more expansive view of the role they play and the places in which they play it. The anchor institutions – the universities, colleges, hospitals, research organisations, and football clubs – must continue to develop ways of working and delivering together. Attitudes and values will be as important to future success as institutions and tools. Trust is crucial to successful city working. It is growing in Liverpool, but more will be needed. A key message of this book is that the city and its people should also have confidence in their future. The job is not yet done. There is more to do and further to go. But the experience of the past thirty years demonstrates that adversity can be overcome. The city's challenges have been, can be and will be met.

Is the post-imperial city yet remade?

At the beginning of this book I argued that Liverpool had fallen from an imperial city to become a post-imperial city, and that it was still coming to terms with this. I argued that its imperial past had shaped the place and its people hugely, affecting its scale, reach, size, economic and social structure, politics, culture and attitudes. The imperial city was extroverted; globally connected; economically, culturally and socially diverse; self-confident and adventurous. But pre- and post-war economic shocks went against it so that many of those characteristics and virtues were challenged and lost. The city became a shadow of its former self economically, politically, socially, culturally and demographically. Economically it lost its role and self-confidence. Physically it imploded and disintegrated as it lost almost half its population. Politically it became introverted and resentful. This book has shown that the fall was real and serious and that the place and its people developed self-doubt. But it has also shown that the place, its leaders and its people have emerged from those shadows and found a new self-belief. It will never again be – and nor should it be – an imperial city. But the post-imperial city has found a way. It is being remade. It is growing in self-confidence. It is raising its aspirations and its horizons. Liverpool does matter. It is well beyond the brink. I finished *Liverpool on the Brink* by saying the saga was 'a Greek tragedy. Its fate was determined as the play opened. The actors merely made sure it met it.' But that is no longer true. That is the significance of the city's renaissance. The actors in the current Liverpool play are actively writing a new ending. And it's not a tragedy.

Notes

1   Quoted in Parkinson and Lord, op. cit., p. 3.

2   LCR LEP, *Summary Internationalisation Strategy and Delivery Plan* (2018).

3   Michael Parkinson, *The Liverpool Brand: What Is It and Why Is It so Important Today?* (Heseltine Institute, University of Liverpool, 2017).

4   Nick Kavanagh, *Transformational Regeneration* (Liverpool City Council, 2017).

5   Liverpool City Council, *Ten Streets Spatial Regeneration Framework* (2017).

6   Liverpool City Region, *A Science and Innovation Audit*, report to BEIS (2017).

7   Liverpool City Council and Sefton Borough Council, *A Strategic Regeneration Framework for North Liverpool* (2010).

8   Liverpool City Council, *Liverpool Maritime Mercantile City* (Liverpool University Press, 2005).

9   State of Liverpool City Region Report, op. cit., p. 78.

10 Paul Kyprianou, *Getting By* (Liverpool City Council Action Group on Poverty, 2015).

11 Michael Parkinson, 'An Urban Legend: The Renaissance of Boston', *New Society*, 9 October 1987.

12 Mayor of Liverpool, *Inclusive Growth Plan – A Strong and Growing City Built on Fairness* (Liverpool City Council, 2018).

13 Paul Sissons, Anne E. Green and Kevin Broughton, 'Inclusive Growth in English Cities: Mainstreamed or Sidelined?', *Regional Studies*, DOI: 10.1080/00343404.2018.1515480 (accessed 26 December 2018).

14 Liverpool City Council, *Liverpool City Centre Strategic Investment Framework* (2012).

15 Baltic Creative, *Annual Report 2016–17* (2017).

16 Liverpool City Council, *Ten Streets Spatial Regeneration Framework*.

Index